D0121246

Enjoying Later Life

Elspeth Jackman

Onwards and Upwards Publishers, Berkeley House,
11 Nightingale Crescent, West Horsley, Surrey KT24 6PD

www.onwardsandupwards.org

copyright © Elspeth Jackman 2012

The right of Elspeth Jackman to be identified as the author of this work has been asserted by the author in accordance with the Copyright, Designs and Patents Act 1988.

All rights reserved.

No part of this publication may be reproduced or transmitted in any form or by any means, electronic or mechanical, including photocopy, recording or any information storage and retrieval system, without permission in writing from the author or publisher.

Scriptures and additional materials quoted are from the Good News Bible © 1994 published by the Bible Societies/HarperCollins Publishers Ltd UK, Good News Bible © American Bible Society 1966, 1971, 1976, 1992. Used with permission.

Type set: Garamond 14

ISBN: 978-1-907509-44-5
Cover design: Leah-Maarit

Printed in the UK

Dedication

To my late husband
David Radclyffe Jackman

Enjoying Later Life

Contents

Enjoying Later Life

Foreword by Pam Rhodes

Elspeth encourages us all to think of later life as a glorious opportunity to celebrate everything we are, everything God knows us to be! Her advice is a beguiling mixture of practical advice and spiritual celebration, along with a healthy dose of humour, a pragmatic approach to health and ill health, tolerance and understanding about situations and people we can't change or control - and a determination that in body, mind and soul we make every moment count!

- PAM RHODES, MARCH 2012 -

"This is a jewel; such simple practical wisdom given in a friendly, non-judgmental way."

David Payne
Director of Catholic Faith Exploration (CaFE)

Prologue

This book is very personal. What suits me may not suit you at all. However, I have what I would say is a very 'sticky ear'. I am always on the look-out for tips on how to do 'later life' in a better, more glorious way. So a lot of the ideas are not mine at all, but I have picked them up from a variety of sources and experimented with them and in some cases, made them my own.

So I offer you this book of what I have discovered and taken to myself. If you are appalled at anything I suggest, then go away and think up your way of dealing with the situation, and write a book of your own. I'll buy it, read it and get even more out of my later life.

Happy reading!

- ELSPETH JACKMAN -

Enjoying Later Life

1

You Now

Transformation story

It actually doesn't matter that much what you have been like up to now. As to the future, that's yet to come, but what is important is what you are NOW. You are created in the image of God. You are being transformed by the renewing of your mind (Romans 12:2). Like a tree whose leaves stay green you are to be fruitful in old age (Psalm 92:12-14). God is a potter re-forming you.

"We are the clay, you are the potter. We are all the work of your hand."(Isaiah 64:8)

God has been working on you for years. He's proud of you. You are not winding down - the world thinks that. You are coming to a culmination of fruitfulness... get your mind set on that!

What God expects of an 80 year old is just as much as a 70 year old but different and the same goes for a 60 year old. Look back! See when you were first interested in God, when you were born again, filled with the Spirit, moved on in a spiritual area, had a breakthrough, encouraged someone to be curious about the claims of Jesus, had prophecies for people, received a healing or were part of a healing. Write down a spiritual time line of the positives and leave the negative to the psychiatrists.

You might look back with longing on the time with a loved one that has now gone. That's not wrong. You might look back with longing to a different period when top of your wish list was more of God, more of his Spirit in your life, more of the joy of Jesus and opportunities to talk about it. That's also not wrong but it's something you can change in the present.

If there are negatives, decide once and for all to leave behind anything that has put you down. You now are part of the Church, the beautiful Bride. You in your weakness and failure and possibly failing health are really glorious in God's sight. He sees Jesus in you and loves you now, whether you are 64 or 94.

Jane Fonda calls this time the '3rd Act' of your life:

"when the empathetic, sensitive aspects of your psyche can make a comeback, allowing your final decades to be happier and relationships healthier."

How much more should we, as Christians believe that the best wine is that which has matured for a long time?

Anna

In the Bible there's one elderly lady who has an important part in the story of Jesus: Anna. I'm not sure that 1st century men and women lived as long as we do. I know there are more people aged over 60 than any other age group in this 21st century. I'll just quote the passage in the Good News version of the Bible.

"There was a very old prophet, a widow named Anna, daughter of Phanuel of the tribe of Asher. She had been married for only seven years and was now 84 years old. She never left the Temple, fasting and praying. That very same hour she arrived and gave thanks to God and spoke about the child to all who were waiting for God to set Jerusalem free."

What a woman! She recognised this one baby, presented at the temple as the promised Messiah. Now there must have been a continual stream of mums and babies. We tend to forget children in the Jewish worship system of New Testament ways. She watched child after child being brought into the temple for circumcision, but she was so intimate with God that she knew in her spirit that this Jesus was the One that all the Jews were waiting for.

She probably had grandchildren of her own, as she would have had children in her seven years of marriage, but this baby was even more special to her. Believing that she had seen the Messiah was the culmination of her spiritual life. It was not only a significant moment for her, it was a significant moment for the millions of us down the ages who have believed in Jesus, as it was included in Luke's account of his life. 'For such a time of this' did Anna appear on the scene, and at 80! What a vindication of the spiritual significance of the older woman.

God's words of encouragement

If you are a regular reader of the Bible you will find a lot of words to encourage you as you enjoy later life. Here's a choice one - it's from Proverbs 16:31.

"Long life is the reward of the righteous; grey hair is a glorious crown."

Yes and the Psalms! Just look at Psalm 92, for instance, that I've already touched on - verse 12 and 14. "The righteous will flourish like palm trees; they will grow like the cedars of Lebanon. They are like trees planted in the house of the Lord, that flourish in the Temple of our

God, that still bear fruit in old age, and are always green and strong."

We should be taking those words to heart. We should be pinning them to our doorposts if not our foreheads, like the Jewish people do with their mezuzas. Do you want to bear fruit in your later years? Do you want to always be green and strong in spirit even if your body wears out a bit? It is possible. Believe it!

I heard a story of a new resident of a care home. She was probably in her early eighties.

"Do come and join the others in the lounge," invited the care assistant.

"Oh no dear," responded the newcomer, "I don't want to go there. They are all old people in the lounge."

Until recently an elderly friend of mine used to walk me, until I was tired, through the London streets to the Royal Academy for their Summer Exhibition. She used to work there at one time and was on speaking terms with L.S. Lowrie (him and his greasy hat) and Stanley Spencer. She belongs to a very active local Anglican church, and confessed to me recently that when the church decided to run a folk dance society, her heart leapt inside her, knowing she'd love to join. She then realised that although she felt 25, she could not move like a 25 year old, and was quite disappointed.

But my advice to you who feel eternally youthful - and why should we not as we are moving on into eternity after our bodies wear out - my advice is: Please don't spend time looking at your wrinkles; after all, most of them are laughter lines. Instead let the smile of God within you beam out. People will notice your youthful attitude which has its source within you.

2

Dealing with Past Hurts and Embarrassments

Anyone writing about later in life or old age will talk about the need to do something about those parts of your life that still hurt a little or that still make you embarrassed.

Secular views

For instance, in the Big Issue June 2011, (a good source for honest comment), the non-Christian Simon Honore writes:

"We cannot liberate humanity if we have not freed ourselves from the addictions that endanger us. We cannot bring harmony to the world if there is none in our lives. History shows that so often people set out with high ideals but fall victim to their weaknesses and the unresolved issues inside them."

Simon talks of transforming the hurt in our lives to forgiveness and compassion and he says that the way we live each day forms part of the subtle atmosphere that affects us on this earth. That perceptive view was from somebody who did not believe in the proverbial 'pie in the sky when you die' either.

Again, Marie de Hennezel in her book 'The Warmth of the Heart Prevents your Body from Rusting' suggests that you unravel the wool of your life, untangling all the knots and making it into a ball, going through all the events of your life one by one and dealing with them.

Jane Fonda writes in similar vein:

"While we cannot undo what has been, we can change the way we understand and feel about it, and this changes everything. It helps us decommission our demons, frees us from the past and gives us a boost as we go forward into the rest of our lives."

She says she replaced stress with detachment, not indifference, but "rather an ability to observe events with greater objectivity, fairness and perception instead of all that subjectivity."

These secular writers, I understand, sadly did not have access to the understanding that there is a way to deal with past hurts. Marie, though a therapist, did not have a way of blotting out the darker parts of our life. In other words, past hurts and sins that come up could not be finally dealt with, just discussed. This is where Christians have such a trump card. Oh the freedom to get rid of guilt in Jesus, even if we haven't dealt with the issues as they came up in our past life!

If your thoughts turn often to sadder parts of the past... or those embarrassing moments, or times when you have made a mistake, ask Jesus to cleanse your mind, to bring healing through the power of the Holy Spirit so that all the baggage you have unwittingly been carrying is off-loaded. If you are brave enough, seek out a mature person who is experienced in helping people be free of past burden, and ask them to facilitate the Holy Spirit's work in you.

One of my friends is a missionary in Vienna, who works in the area of freeing people in this way, which is sometimes called the Deliverance Ministry. She lives in a flat in central Vienna and I well remember her recounting to me that she decided to be really direct with God.

"Look God," she said, "I live in a flat. There are people above me and below me and next to me. I really can't be doing with any shouting, when people are delivered, and freed."

And so it is that when someone comes for prayer with her, she hardly speaks a word, and her client is usually quiet, but as she prays inwardly, then difficult or shameful moments in the client's past come into his or her mind, and my friend is able then to ask what has come up, and very gently and authoritatively free the person. I know this, because just praying with her casually I found this happening to me.

You may not think you need deliverance, or freeing from anything or you might object to the mention of evil spirits, but this interaction is not a moment of shame and condemnation, it's a time for being renewed and become pure and whole. You may have put many issues in your 'deleted items' box but you might not have emptied your 'recycle bin'!

Perhaps you left one church and joined another, and the hurts that you experienced were deep. After a while you decided that you must forgive the people concerned, and you even confessed your sins and forgave them in the presence of a friend or mentor you trust. You have deleted these items.

However, from time to time, the 'niggles' and hurt re-surfaces and you realise you need an even deeper work of the Spirit to clean you out thoroughly. I am convinced that the redemptive power of Jesus on the Cross can also deal with these hurts so that you move in new dependence on Jesus and the power of his Spirit. Now you will have emptied your recycle bin of those deleted items. There are things to do practically as well. You have forgiven those who hurt you, so you must not blame them again or recite the story to someone else for sympathy. (I've done this to my shame). You have also been forgiven for the things you have done wrong or the words that you shouldn't have said.

"If we confess our sin he is faithful and just to forgive us our sins and purify us from all wrong doing" (I John 1:9).

We also need to forgive ourselves, especially for our mistakes. God even deals with our mistakes. I used to beat myself up about embarrassing moments as well which is probably my pride at not wanting to look a fool. He can get rid of the pangs that you feel when a 'film-clip' of certain scenes from the past flicks into your mind, although I personally find this harder than obvious wrong doing.

At our age, you and I have many more years behind us, so we have the possibility of a lot more shameful and hurtful things that could pop into our minds. Ask for cleaning out by Jesus... and when the enemy tries to sow a seed tell him where to go.

I find that in the night I wake up and think things I shouldn't, so sometimes I put on the radio. Premier Christian Radio is good, or you might choose Radio 4 or another favourite. We need to use whatever stratagems we have to take our minds off bad thoughts. Read the words of Scripture to yourself out loud. Jesus himself, when tempted, told the devil where to go by saying, "It is written."

I just love the verse, "There is no condemnation for those who are in Christ Jesus," from the Book of Romans chapter 8.

We will naturally have more time on our own than younger people. Therefore there is more time for those unwanted recollections to come to the surface of our minds. We have all switched on the TV or gone to the fridge to blot out hurting thoughts, but how good to get the root of them plucked out, never to come back.

Then the story Jesus told comes to mind. One devil is sent out of a man, and his inner house is clean and swept, but then seven more come to inhabit it.

We need to replace the bad thoughts with good ones. As a contingency plan, it might be an idea to have worked out set phrases, perhaps quotes from the Bible, to deal with each hurt that is just on the edge of entering in. This will mean that we can speak out the positives with our minds and our voices so that the house is occupied, as it were, and no devils can come back in.

For example, if the thought of a child being sexually abused, then murdered, comes into your mind to bother you, consider the fictional story in THE SHACK, where the three persons of the Godhead, shown as human people, assured the dad that they were whispering comfort and peace in his daughter's ears, and they took away the pain, as she was abused and murdered.

Forgiveness

Past hurts may not, however, be those shadows lurking from the long, lost past. You could have been hurt yesterday. If there is one lesson that I have found hard to learn it is that I should be quick to forgive. Part of each one of us wants to indulge and almost relish in the hurtful words or deeds that were perpetrated against us. We almost think that we can hug this justified resentment for several days, and then perhaps we'll move on. I have done that. However, if I want to know the presence of Jesus with me, and the peace of God upon me, I have to school myself to forgive quickly.

I've recently taken part in an OPEN STUDIOS scheme, whereby any artist can open their home when they choose, over a 6-week period, under the auspices of a county-wide Visual Arts Forum, which produces a brochure including everyone's times of opening, and a coloured picture of a sample of their work.

This was my first time, so I was assiduous in informing people by email, phone, article, radio 'plug' and so on. They were invited to a 'cuppa' and a chance to view my work and see how I created my pictures. I think my expectations were too high, as very few people came, but I had been invited to put two pictures into a nearby separate Christian exhibition alongside someone else's Open Studio. So I carefully created a card flyer including pictures, saying, 'And now come to Elspeth's Open Studios half a mile away', with all details.

The other day I received my pictures back again and in the bottom of the bag were my promotional flyers. They hadn't even been put out.

I wanted to sulk and tell everyone I'd been hard done by, but the continued flow of the Holy Spirit was more important to me, so I made myself forgive this lovely lady, (nearly) straight away.

It's the little grievances that can spoil our well-being, like a drop of ink in a jar of water. I have to - we have to - put these things behind us and resist the powerful temptation to share are pains with our friends.

Besides being hurt and hurting others, there are other 'flies in the ointment'. I'm talking about mistakes we make. These are not crimes, not sins, but due perhaps either to a moment of foolishness or genuine ignorance.

I find that these will cause a lot of unease and the absence of peace. I haven't usually done anyone else any harm. I've either wasted a bit of money, or time, and I'm not pleased with myself. At this point I should be telling myself that God knows my frailty, he is kind, and he is just laughing it off. I have to forgive myself.

Quite often my focus on one job in the house is lost when another attracts me and that often causes burnt toast. I have a sharp sense of smell so I usually get to the grill just as the smoke alarm is sounding off, and I only lose a slice of bread, and gain the cold air from outside when I have to open the back door, and a smelly hall and kitchen. I think I was fortunate the other day as I boiled a kettle of water by electricity but did not replace the lid, and by the time I'd arrived on the scene, all the water was everywhere but in the kettle, and I was exceedingly glad I hadn't actually killed my lovely new (half price at a sale) expensive-looking kettle.

Then there are the items I've ordered on line or through a mail order catalogue and didn't check all the details. I thought that a half 'car cover' would be a boon and a good alternative to scraping the ice off my car windscreen, but I hadn't checked the size, and it was massively too big for my little Ford Ka.

I make mistakes in many areas. Near St Albans, where I live, is a five exit roundabout. It was dark. I knew I needed to take the third exit to get to the theatre. However, for some reason I got muddled and took the second exit. It led into a motorway and it took me 10 minutes of fast driving to find a place to turn round, and then another ten minutes back again. I can laugh about it now. I must cultivate the habit of smiling sooner. This is where chatting with friends is a great help.

I suppose in a way, we have to expect that we miss the mark unintentionally at times. If we have hurt others by mistake, we can apologise and ask their forgiveness, which actually are two different things. If we have just done a foolish thing and inconvenienced ourselves we must determine to leave it behind and live in joy!

3

Thankfulness

Make thankfulness a conscious thing!

Do you remember the 'glad game' of Pollyanna in the 1913 novel by Eleanor H. Porter? Pollyanna was the daughter of missionaries and every year she would look forward to the missionary barrel of donated presents. The glad game was created when she was extremely disappointed not to find a doll but a pair of crutches. Her father's response was to say, "Well, let's be glad about the crutches because we don't need 'em!" So this odd little character used to make a game of being glad for everything. Reading the book I thought her a prig at the time, but there is a truth behind the story.

Corrie ten Boom was an amazing Dutch Christian lady who used to shelter Jews and hide them in her home in the time of Hitler's Holocaust. Eventually her deeds were discovered and she and her sister were put in a concentration camp. However she insisted that they gave thanks in all circumstances and for everything. At one point their shed got infested with fleas.

"You can't give thanks for fleas," cried her sister. "Oh yes I can," retorted Corrie and proceeded to do so. What actually happened was indeed in the prisoners' favour. The warders came to know that their hut had fleas, and so avoided it completely. The inmates were free from visits and intervention.

Of course it's much easier to start thanking for all the lovely things we have. I love to gather fresh strawberries and raspberries in the season. I creep outside into the garden in my 'nightie', and add them to my muesli! Breakfast is just what I want it to be and it's lovely. Add to that the bonus of bird song and it isn't hard to give thanks.

I heard the habit of thankfulness called the 'gratitude gym' by Mary Dempsey in her book: '8 Secrets to Amazing Life'. And it is a fun exercise! Okay, you've got to go to the dentist... but give thanks that they have reasonable anaesthetics nowadays... and if you can't share your faith with the dentist because your mouth is fixed open, you can always do it while paying the bill.

After my husband died, now ten years ago, a neighbour gave me a kind of birthday book, but she told me to write in it something I was thankful for every day; and she was not a Christian.

Thankfulness has such a positive effect even on our physical bodies. I'm told there was a survey of people who had the same amount of physical difficulties – from minor ailments to hip replacements. Apparently those questioned who said they were in excellent health had much longer life expectation than those were said that their health was poor.

Speaking out the positive is such a God-given way of keeping in mental and physical health.

I live alone, but I am not reticent about speaking aloud in the privacy of my own home. In the world's eyes speaking to yourself is thought to be a sign of going 'gaga'. On the contrary! I believe it is good to do so. You can speak aloud to Jesus or the Holy Spirit or Father in heaven, or you can just speak out the positive. I see nothing wrong is speaking out a whole chapter of thankfulness. You may not choose to do this is the garden with your neighbour within hearing distance, but here we touch on the importance of words theologically. God created the world by his words. We can affirm biblical truths by speaking out words. We can create a positive framework by our words.

I had my daughter when I was 39 and half years old (having married for the first time at 38). I had high blood pressure and was made to stay in hospital for 'rest'. Hmmph! Well I pleaded (tongue-in-cheek) with the doctors that I had a ballet to review and could I have a double bed please with my husband, but to no avail. So I think I was three weeks there before my Sarah arrived, and it was no rest at all. At night the lights were on, and there was constant activity in the ward. Oh, it was awful! What I remember when I finally came home was the sheer difference of a normal house from a clinically clean hospital ward. There was colour, there was clutter. It was marvellous! Was I thankful!

There's a saying, although I don't know where it came from: 'Two men were behind bars. One looked down and saw mud. The other looked up and saw stars.'

Everything is comparative. I have noticed that young people who spend some weeks in underdeveloped countries come back with a changed outlook on life. The other month I interviewed some teenagers for my Christian radio programme. They had to work at raising money for their trip to Africa. That was hard. Then when they finally arrived in Africa, their task was to build a house. Yes, manual labour: carrying bricks, mixing cement, sawing planks as well as playing with all the children. The food was different, sleeping-quarters rough, but they said their greatest thrill was to see the dad of the family receive the keys to his own house. They came back changed on the inside from experiencing how underprivileged families live on the other side of the world. I don't expect they complained so much at ordinary city life.

Jane Fonda says that her new-found positivity may be due to 'the accumulation of perspective', so that she sees the difficulties and hard times as challenges that can be met and overcome.

Yes, I'm with Mary Dempsey and taking her advice; do your 'gratitude gym' every day! It's one of those exercises that encourage you to start saying words that express thankfulness, even though you don't always feel thankful always. The spirit of thankfulness will clothe the structure of your spoken thanks. We come back time and time again to the fact that God created through his Word. Our words can create a spirit of praise even within ourselves.

4

Rhythm

Music is part of the warp or weft of every life. I do a radio programme like a 'desert island discs' show, where my guest chooses significant pieces of music from his or her life. We have the regulars... the Beatles, Simon and Garfunkel, Elvis, Queen, the Kinks. I discovered that many people collect thousands of tracks and live for their music quiz each week. There's such a breadth to it. I remember queuing up for the 'Proms' in my student days to stand and enjoy live orchestral music. Contemporary Christian music was in its infancy, with short Bible choruses for young people, and Songs of Fellowship music, blossoming with the first house churches. I played the piano and as a teenager was a very rough and mediocre musician, though I've turned into an able piano teacher who understands those who are slow to learn. We've all had our own experiences of music throughout lives.

There's music for every mood... gentle sound that is a pleasant background for studying... praise music to uplift you.... Grand Opera to draw out deep emotions... general Pop to keep your day afloat.

However I reckon that every piece of music you enjoy has a pattern, a rhythm; it might be calypso or it might be marching music, as in brass bands that I've watched on TV in the Edinburgh Tattoo. It might be the Viennese Waltz from 'Strictly Come Dancing'; it might be the heavy thunder of Punk.

Not many of us enjoy the strange compositions of classical music where there's hardly a tune to be heard; just unexpected sounds in different patterns at different intervals.

Well, I understand from this that God enjoys rhythm. How did mankind come to mark the passages of time in the beginning? The account of God's creation of the world talks in terms of days, but that was the author's concept.

We are comfortable with living a day at a time, with a night to release us into a gap period so that we can start afresh each day.

We see the patterns of the seasons... we expect roses in June and daffodils in April... we expect fog and snow in the winter months in Britain... and it would be a very different world if every day we had the same climate and the same growth (although we have the same produce in the shops).

So I conclude that we are created to enjoy patterns, to enjoy rhythm in our lives. Therefore, in handling our own personal lives, we are bound to be more comfortable in some sort of rhythm of life.

Now in case you think I am advocating living in a rut, think again. When every single thing - every relationship, every event - changes every other day, we are surely longing for stability of some sort, a thread on which to thread all these different beads.

I am suggesting that habit, good habit, is a very good thing. Think about your day!

What about finding things. Is it not easier if you always put your bunch of keys in the same place? My late husband used to 'go spare' over mislaying his glasses case, never mind his glasses. And it's usually the important things you need to refer to immediately, that you keep somewhere special, and don't put away in their correct drawer or the right file and can't find when you need them. In later life, it's all a bit simpler if you have regular places for everything. Let's face it - our forgetting is often stronger than our memory at times.

Security checking

Oh yes, and that brings me on to another allied subject. Often, when I'm in the car having just left the house - half a mile away is usual - a nasty thought comes to my mind, "you left the gas on" or "you didn't lock the front door" are some of the regulars. So to counter them, as I know myself by now, and I try to say aloud as I lock up or check that the gas is turned off, "I have locked the car, I have checked the kitchen."

I remember once that our daughter was playing in a Trinity College concert on her violin and that meant me going down to London. David, my husband, had gone earlier and I was taking a tube down after my own piano teaching. Well, I left the car in the station car park, got the tube and even when I'd just sat down, realised that I could not remember actually locking the car door. Now if you believe in spiritual warfare at all, you could say that the devil had a field day. Do you recall in the list of the part of spiritual armour in Ephesians 6, the command is to hold up the shield of faith 'to counter any sharp barbs that the devil might inflict on us'? I certainly didn't enjoy that journey down. Imagine having to say to my husband "I'm so, so sorry the car's been stolen; I didn't lock it." Happily, on the programme was a choral number to some beautiful scriptural words and one sentence was, "There is no condemnation to those who are in Christ Jesus," and I hung onto that and clung to it throughout the concert. I didn't mention my thoughts to David and Sarah, but I went quite speedily to check my car. Yes I had locked it!

There was another instance. I was being picked up by another member of a Christian organisation to go to a house party in Bournemouth for Easter. Oh yes, the delight of not having to drive! I had made sure that everything, just everything, was locked and off, from my microwave to my TV, though I was only going for a long weekend. However, I had been watering my garden earlier and half way down to Bournemouth realised that I couldn't remember the action of turning off the outside tap.

It stayed with me. I had no peace. The devil or one his henchman must have been cavorting with glee. So I rang my friend and then texted her just in case she and her husband could pop around and peep over the wall and see if water was cascading everywhere. I stupidly had not taken my neighbour's phone number. No answer. We went to dinner. No answer. Then at 9:00pm I got a call. As it was Good Friday, my friend had not had her mobile on. Anyway, it was getting dark, but they said they would drive round, and oh dear, they had to get through a prickly hedge wondering if people would think they were burglars, and of course - NO WATER HAD BEEN LEFT RUNNING. I owe a great debt of gratitude to these friends who put themselves out for me.

So, you may not be like me, but ALWAYS CHECK EVERYTHING, saying it aloud. We usually do the correct thing automatically, and therefore we don't retain it in our memory. Whew! I MUST LEARN this lesson. Checking must be built into the rhythm of my life.

Eating habits

What about other facets of your day? You must know that your body functions better if it's fed at more or less the same time each day, with the usual consequences at the usual times. You may want to splurge out on late night parties and the occasional difference is fun. Belonging to an Operatic Society, I found that in show week, when we were on stage every night, Friday was always curry night, and the cast would go after the show and eat curry together. I'm sure it was excellent socially, but curry at 11:15pm? My elderly digestive system had got too set in its ways to contemplate that!

Our bodies are amazing and adaptable, and only when a minute thing goes wrong do we notice how complicated the whole thing called 'me' is.

What about sleep patterns? For us women who've probably gone through nights of insomnia due to the changes in our hormones, we should be able to take sleep patterns in our stride. In later life, we might wake up regularly at say three or four in the morning. If that's the case don't moan but let's see this as a brief interlude and work on ways to get ourselves back to sleep.

I'm talking about the rhythm of life here, but I do want to come back later to the subject of sleep regarding our minds and what they dream about, or waking up thinking about, or can't help dwelling on!

Do you find you need less sleep when you are of a mature age? I do. I know Margaret Thatcher was famous for her short nights and her insatiable brain beavering away at five in the morning. I have my clock set up to wake me at a certain time but it's a rare morning when I reach that time.

Before we had artificial light, people followed the rhythm of the seasons in their sleeping and woke with the dawn. That does of course mean that they worked more in the summer. But again, God gave rhythm into this life, and apart from some delightful exceptions, we'll be much more satisfied if we, too, have a usual pattern of sleep and waking.

Oh yes, and do you submit to a nap after lunch? One of the scenes from my childhood was of our kitchen on an early Sunday afternoon. The rest of us did the washing up, often to the radio, (remember the Glums?) but my mother would sit at the table, put her head down on her arms and go to sleep just like that, and be refreshed after about 10 minutes. You could promote the theory that you'll sleep better at night if you don't sleep in the day. Or you could say that to be fresh to tackle afternoon jobs, you need just a few minutes asleep! Up to you, but I know that your body will enjoy a pattern, the rhythm of whatever you choose to do.

So then, what about the rhythm of what we do in the day? Yes, we all enjoy our 'to do' lists. It gives such satisfaction crossing off the jobs we need to do.

But let me ask: Does your rhythm include different melodies at this time? I have long worked out that in this life for me there are necessary things and there are important things. You have to do your grocery shopping. You have to have your hair done; you have to get your meals ready; you have to do your washing; you have to cut the lawn. Yes, I find a rhythm to those types of jobs really helpful. I now cut mine once a week - my lawn that is - not my hair! Yes, it's Friday - time to cut the lawn! I mentioned it to my neighbour and he said he cut it when it needed it.

The necessary things have to be done. However, if these are the flagstaffs in your life, the poles around which other things must come in line, then may I suggest that you need a little more sparkle in your life? Please, please don't grow old looking forward to the shopping, the hair do, and getting the house clean. These all have their place, but people are important too. What are important things in your life? Do you look forward to seeing your grand-children? Do you have the challenge of writing an article for the parish magazine? Do you ever write to the local paper because you feel strongly about something?

I very rarely write to our local paper, but when I have done, it is astonishing how many people had read what I said. I was championing the 'Big Issue' vendor in the market place, who was a Christian and with a wife and young family on very little income. I wanted the people in St. Albans to support him for the sake of £2 a week, and perhaps forgo the Starbucks coffee for once.

Another part of the rhythm of life should involve the spiritual part of us and a very old fashioned term – 'spiritual disciplines'.

There's an old fashioned term called the 'quiet time'. Anyone remember it? Long ago, when we became committed to Jesus Christ, we were told that we needed to read the Bible and pray every day and this was best in the morning and you called it your quiet time. In those days too, it was the 'done thing' to kneel by your bed to pray.

Well, whatever we call it now, most Christians believe it is extremely important for us to keep a time each day set aside for God to meditate in his presence, to plan the day with him, to enjoy being fed (yes its bread and milk and honey) by reading the Bible. Then you need time to intercede for others. You can wield a lot of power through the Spirit by praying for other people. Is this part of your rhythm? If you sleep in a room on your own, there is no reason at all why this should not be part of your daily pattern of life.

It sets you up for the day. Also, it may bring things to mind you need to act on in the day, so that although its 'mowing the lawn' day or 'doing the washing' day, you know you need to pop round to that friend instead because she's feeling really down at the moment. And how do you know to do *that*? Because you have had a sort of debriefing with your Maker! You have put the days' events in his hands and are open to suggestions that come from him. The presence of Jesus is with you in a fuller way and usually the ideas that come to you then are from God.

I find that God is brilliant at reminding me of things I ought to do that are not on my TO DO list. Recently I had been struggling to order some cheap CD's on the internet but saw that there was £6 postage, and really wanted free delivery,

I'd even asked a kind friend who helps me with computer problems to come round and I was going to consult with her. However, I woke up that morning and realised that, of course, I'd found the task easy last time. And why? Because I had rung up! So one phone call got me quicker to where I wanted than 15 minutes of trying to search the internet site!

Andy Hickford, in 'Christianity' May 2011, in an article concerning the consumer culture, wrote, "If we are to live free, if we are to live the life God intended for us and not be seduced by consumerism's snare, we have to learn to train, practising the rhythms, disciplines and habits that will sustain our life in Christ in what is effectively the enemy-occupied territory of consumer culture."

So let's implement God's idea of rhythm into our own lives. At our age, so much is in our own hands. We do not have to get the children off to school, clear up the breakfast, and dash out to work ourselves. Let's co-operate with God in this, listening to the rhythm he wants us to enjoy, and allowing his life in us to burst out in any way he wants to, even temporarily changing our usual patterns of living.

5

What You See Influences You

When I started looking for my first house I thought I would enjoy most places. I was not fussy, I told myself. Then when I found one house with the only toilet the other side of the kitchen, and another house, where every window looked out onto a brick wall about 3 feet away, I found I was extremely particular.

In this current financial climate, any dwelling, boxed in, with outside toilet, right next to a factory, or a noisy pub could be our own special home. We'd be so fortunate to have it.

However, I am several houses into adult life, and I am so privileged just now. I am continually thankful that I wake up, go downstairs and on the way down, glance out of the window and see horses! Horses, yes! There's also a busy road but I happen to have a small paddock opposite my house and three living prancing horses are always there. There's a grey-blue dappled one tossing his mane, a small, obstinate, squat pony called Obie, eating his way into trouble, and a soft-eyed brown one. The area I live in is constantly threatened by at least four planning proposals, but it is named 'semi-rural', and at the moment it lives up to its name.

I also just love the look of my garden through the windows. At the back, my house may look quite pedestrian, with three large flat windows upstairs and three large ones downstairs, but from the inside, the view is like a tonic. I teach piano several hours a day, and if the pupil's playing is a little boring I glance past their fingers to the bird table outside, usually populated with tits, finches and more. When I wake in the morning, I revel at the skyline seen from my bed and my gigantic apple tree which I suppose I should get pruned, now in competition with the cherry tree. There are the dark green fingers of the juniper which is creeping quite swiftly across my lawn to divide up the garden, and the brilliant yellow choisya which I started in a barrel mid-lawn to break up the expanse. Just now there are hollyhocks, self-seeded in the cracks between the paving slabs, and... I could go on... I can just see the top of the silver birch at the end of the garden and I revel in the visual beauty from where I am. Yes, I am indeed fortunate!

However, not all of us are so fortunate. Some of us live without views of trees, flowers or the countryside.

I want to suggest that as what we see is so important, there are ways of changing our surroundings; and not by moving house either. Why not be a bit radical!

Create your own visual surrounds

Why not go extravagant and choose gorgeous plants or maybe a small palm tree? What about cordon apples, or magnolia to climb a wall, or clematis? If you don't have the imagination to dream up your green scenario, bring in a friend. If it's a fence that borders a dark garden, get it painted white or green! What you see around you in your normal daily life does affect you. Make it a visual scenario that you enjoy!

I've just recently been buying more flowers for inside. I just love fresh flowers, particularly the scented variety. Sadly, about twenty years ago I acquired an allergy to perfume, so I really crave natural aromas in the home.

Here's a thought. Are you passionate about the seaside? Be daring and get one wall painted with your favourite seaside scene, whether it be Clacton or the Bahamas. Here's a more up-to-date alternative: You can get electronic viewers that show a rolling view of your favourite photos. Get one as big as a television and enjoy yourself.

Imagination and ideas and a small amount of money will take you into a lot of pleasure, and we should not be marking the last third or quarter of our life at half-cock, relapsing into drabness with the excuse that we haven't the money to do anything better. Have what you really want and ignore what other people say about your taste. Of course, having said that, if you are totally set in your ways and just love it as it has always been, then so be it.

A lot of our time may be spent in our homes as we're not out taking the children to school and back, and we may not be in a full time job, so where we are matters a lot. Some people like to have photos of their family around them: there's the graduation photos, the wedding photos, the anniversary photos. Each glance brings shared moments of love. A cousin of mine keeps about twenty framed family photos displayed on an old chest.

Take a fresh look at your home

Then why not take a fresh look at the rest of your house. If you are a widow, do you want to keep your husband's things as he used them, almost as a shrine to him? I am fortunate to live near Codicote and the house of George Bernard Shaw called Shaw's Corner. Visiting it is a lovely experience, going back in time to the 1930's and 40's, seeing the playwright's study exactly as it was when he was there, as if he had just put down his pen and used his blotting paper.

However, life moves on, and most people retain the joy of their loved ones through memories and a few choice items which bring back the past. This is not the land of Du Maurier's 'Rebecca', where the housekeeper kept everything in the room exactly as her murdered mistress/lover had left it.

I firmly believe that what you see and take in each day is important to your 'joie de vivre'. Has the wall been a dull ochre/brown as long as you have known it? Try for a change. No, you don't need to change the colours around you but you might like new visual surroundings. Look at the many make-over programmes on television. Visit furniture stores. Do a little dreaming. Even the re-arrangement of the furniture you have, and one tin of paint to colour one wall will bring fresh life to keep your life fresh.

I remember in our first house together my husband and I were always going to do up our big and interesting kitchen (complete with pull-up clothes rack). At one point when waiting for the moment and the money to do the big thing, I thought, "Why don't I just paint the walls white?" And a few hours later, the transformation was amazing! Ever after we called the act of doing something immediately, rather than waiting to do it perfectly later, 'painting the kitchen white'.

Be discerning over keeping heir looms

Think of the ornaments and other stuff jumbled over those surfaces. Now don't worry, I'm not going to preach de-cluttering. I get it from a lot of sources. But do you really enjoy the shape of that particular vase or do you only suffer it because your husband's aunt passed it on? Keep the items you love. Keep the items that are special to you by their significance, but if you only keep something because it's an heirloom and you don't actually like it, get help to sell it on 'ebay'. I go to my sisters and brother's houses, and I notice that a lot of what is on their sideboards and dressers I remember from my childhood. Be discerning. Keep what you love. Don't just keep it because it belonged to your parents.

When we were first married, my husband David gave me a present which is still my delight. It's just a large pebble, painted with the face of a cat. I just love it. He said that a girl in the office was selling them and I think he was surprised how much I was thrilled by it. I keep it on my dressing table. It delights me, and the fact that my dear husband gave it to me are two valid reasons for giving it a home.

In my 'singleness' home I had a Jerusalem thorn in a pot. It was a particularly prickly plant, but had a long season of brilliant scarlet flowers. Although I now forget when I first bought it, it was a very special part of my home. Then came the time when we pooled our furniture and effects, and I got the idea that David didn't really like this plant. So I let it go. However, my dear husband must have sensed the sacrifice, because some months later when we saw the plant at a garden centre – a smaller version - he bought it for me, so my earlier love was reinstated.

Make changes the do-it-yourself way, it's cheaper

Is your kitchen sink too high and now you're fed up with it? Get a small stool. Would you like a new bathroom but can't afford six thousand pounds? Decided on a delicious colour and paint the walls yourself, even if you are not a good decorator.

I have a studio for my broadcasting work, and it's filled with microphones, the mixing desk and all the equipment, plus the computer and a keyboard. One day I did a programme with an expert in interior design. Apparently this 'desert island disc' type of programme brought her in quite a bit of work, so as a thank you she offered to help me redesign my room. (And she normally charges £80 per hour!) I took on board some of her ideas. We decided the walls should be green and she gave details of a decorator, who she said would do the room for £150. However, several phone calls later with still no response I asked a decorator friend for a quote. That came to £250 but he asked when could he move all my stuff? I thought about it, realised I needed everything every day, and that I was perfectly capable of squeezing behind the tables and leads and painting it myself. I've done it, at my own convenience. It doesn't look perfect, it's a bit thin in places, but I'm not a perfectionist. I saved money and now I have my own 'green' room.

Life is worth living well NOW

You may think that the pictures on your wall are meant to be there and a permanent part of your decoration. Just as an experiment, change them around, and then go hunting for new ones. I've been amazed that DIY stores even stock large pictures on canvas at very low prices. Buy pictures for your wall. Change your display. Same is familiar. Change is stimulating.

What you watch on television

What do you see on television? Are there things you would like to wipe from your memory? Don't get yourself in the position of watching violence and overt sex. Today it creeps in unawares. Not long ago, admittedly after 10:00pm, Channel 4 TV was showing a programme of advice for teenagers on sex. This sounds reasonable, but I happened to switch on when they were showing clips of a visual of nude actors demonstrating different sexual poses, men with women, men with men. I was almost spellbound and couldn't believe my eyes. Channel 4 is not an adult only channel.

On 'prime time' TV there are always choices to be made. Some Christians may enjoy watching horror films, or working out the evil manifestations in Harry Potter or Merlin. Others may find that their own mind latches and broods on the visual, finding it difficult to throw it off, and for them it is better to look at what is more wholesome. The criteria for our viewing may be different for each of us. I think we ought to be prepared to step out of the mould, whichever way, and see just what we feel God would be pleased for us to see.

Why not do a survey of your television viewing during one week. Write down exactly what you watch and for how long. Then analyse what sort of stuff is going into your visual brain. Of course, there's the fact and fiction in sound going into your brain too, and I am a great advocate of radio, but the visual tends to lodge in your brain for a longer time.

What you hear on radio

Yes, be discerning over radio as well. Once I wasn't very well, (most unusual for me) and I decided to take people's advice and actually rest - that is really difficult for me. I needed to lie down on the bed, without gainful occupation, again an unusual occupation for me. Well, that's when the radio comes into play. But oh dear, there was a play, but homosexuality was a central theme. I changed to another channel and found some sad tales of relationships ending. I switched again and found a documentary on a Hindu family. Nothing could feed me positives, so I switched it off. Then I realised I had in my possession two CD's of the psalms being read to the sound of birdsong and bubbling water and wind etc. Oh, did that feed my soul ! And of course, in another chapter I have written in depth about feeding the soul with God's word.

Look at other people

They say that the eyes are windows to the soul. When you meet someone, how far do you really look at them: the colour of eyes, their hairstyle, their movements, their mannerisms? Do you notice them? Why not draw them in your mind, appreciate them!

Advantage of lack of mobility

One drawback of later life maybe is that we are less mobile than other people, that we are not out every day, walking to the station, standing on the tube, rushing off to work. Maybe, however, this is an advantage. But when I do travel, and I treat myself to 'London days' occasionally just for the stimulation, I find that now I am really fascinated by other people in a way I haven't been before. If you are lucky you obtain a seat in a railway compartment, and though you may have your paper with you, other people - their looks, their habits - are so interesting, plus the view out of the window, that you have all the interest you need. I've seen girls fish out their mirrors and make up and do quite a long intensive job on their face, sitting right next to the executive business man working at his laptop. There are the folk on their mobiles, or those who stare stoically ahead of them. If you work at it you can guess from their eyes where they are, emotionally. You can judge if they are generally disappointed with life, or worried, or frustrated, or angry or at peace. And it's a great time to bring them before God, quietly in your head. I have a much older friend called Betty who says she always prays for people across from her in the tube, and watches God loose the worry from them. Now that is something!

Of course, what you see will be coloured by your attitude. A complaining attitude, a grudge against the world, will not be able to channel the goodness of God. I started off talking of the importance of what we see. Now I'm saying that what we see is important FOR those we see, as we can pray for them.

6

Building Ourselves up with the Food of God's Word

I probably don't have to remind you that God's word is good, good, good for you! I remember a long time ago I used to look forward to Object Sunday when I went to a Bible class as a young teenager: Crusaders. On Object Sunday we could bring any material object that was mentioned in the Bible, and one of the Crusader leaders had to talk briefly about it, drawing out the Christian message. Some people brought such things as coins, pots, and sticks, and some brought items of food, like bread, honey, milk or meat, although I don't recollect the messy ones. Of course for each of those food stuffs you could get a homily on the goodness of God's word, the Bible.

I count myself fortunate to have been brought up in an era when committing yourself to Jesus, meant the QUIET TIME. Yes, it was expected of you. It was a rule that had proved to be so good that it was just understood that you began your day with your quiet time. You would read the Bible, preferably with some notes, and then pray. Now, in this 'free-for-all', 'do–it–if–it–brings–you–instant-fulfilment' age, you won't get strong advice on the morning 'quiet time'. But now it's so inbred into me, that it's just natural, and so good.

On a radio programme Joyce Meyer had a good reply to a woman who said she never remembered what she read in the Bible. "If you put it in, then the Holy Spirit will bring it out." That is, bring it to your mind at the right time.

I've recently got the idea of leaving a Bible open downstairs and pausing in my cleaning, or telly-watching or whatever, just to glance down at a verse I might have underlined, and then to continue my work, mulling it over, and letting it soak into me. The Psalms are particularly good for that.

We who, attempting to enjoy later life, are probably more in the home than we were before, can snack on God's word constantly. His word, we know, is such a morale booster.

For example, feed on Romans chapter 8:1. "There is no condemnation to those who are in Christ Jesus." So in your heart you can respond something like, "Oh God, I said some quick words to my neighbour that I shouldn't have said. I think I might have blown my witness to her. I really repent of that, Lord, and I thank you with all my heart that you have forgiven me, and I am now free from guilt."

His Word is such an encourager. Here's another example: 2 Peter 3:8. "A thousand years is but a day to the Lord." After reading that in your heart you can cry, "Lord I've been praying for this relation for years and she is still far away from wanting a spiritual connection. Thank you that you are outside time, and please give me patience."

When we think no-one else could ever understand how we feel we read, "His understanding is infinite."

Deep in our hearts we know that we must have an enriched diet of his Word to keep our spiritual metabolism in top form. We can't just rely on being fed the truth on Sundays or in the weekly church group. There's also the excitement of reading words that suddenly come alive. You feel they must have been written just for you on that particular occasion. Just for me - does God care that much?

If the Word is rather dry for you, and you've somehow lost your first love for it, just sit down and ask the Holy Spirit to come freshly upon you and give you a great thirst, a great desire for his Word.

The second book of Timothy chapter 2, verse 2, encourages the believer to 'teach others also'. Perhaps our love for God's word could be contagious! Perhaps when others come to our home for this and that, for a cuppa, to trump up 'nimbyism' or whatever, we could share a little of what spoke to us that day from God's word. Perhaps we should use a modern translation. Do remember that God's Word has power in itself and will be retained by the listener.

His Word will remain in your heart and mind when maybe you forget other things. Even now I forget someone's name two minutes after I ask it, if I don't use it again. I think that might be the give-away as to my real age when I'm in company.

I once went to take a weekly Christian session in a day centre for those with special needs. Most of my group were mentally disabled. It was just so lovely that spiritual communication from these people to the mighty God was not impaired in the slightest. Their minds might not be able to take in ordinary material things and concepts, their minds may not be able to bring the right words into their mouths, but their understanding of spiritual issues was second-to-none. This was a very humbling and exhilarating experience as the title of Corrie ten Boom's book says, 'Common Sense Not Needed'.

So, as I write this, new thoughts pour into my mind that I believe are from God. If we have stored up his Word in our hearts, and continue to do so, and revise what we know, and delight in it constantly, then if our mental condition deteriorates, we still have the most important thing and can be constantly enriched by it. So there's great hope for us in our really later life.

7

How Far to Go to Stay Looking Young

I am leaving the subject of exercise to later in this chapter, but each one of us must have ideas on how far we believe the eternal youthfulness of a woman enjoying the fullness of the Holy Spirit should be seen from how we keep our bodies looking good. Have you noticed that there are always ladies in the 60's looking gorgeous and dancing their way to fitness on Strictly Come Dancing? Of course, they have every artifice possible to create that look. What factors influence you in how well groomed you are?

- Is it finance?
- Is it a sense of what is right in God?
- Is it our upbringing?
- Is it peer pressure?

Finance

As Christians we believe that what we receive is put in our hands, entrusted to us to use to his glory in the widest sense. And this is an area where I have to hold my tongue, because for everyone the parameters are different. Some will feel it right to be lavish in some things. Others will think this totally wrong and spend highly in other areas.

I remember that one couple who invited my late husband and I to a meal were very proud that they could offer us home-grown chard from their garden. They boasted how economical it was to serve home-grown food. However, with their rolls was the best better; no butter substitute spreads around.

At one point I was surprised that my daughter had highlights in her hair. "Is this a good use of money of one who is an assistant pastor?" I said to myself. Then I laughed long and hard at myself, as I get my hair coloured every six weeks, to keep away the 'silver surfer' look.

Buying the best?

There used to be the principle held by my parents' generation that you always bought the very best quality of goods that you could afford. This applied especially when you bought clothes. Now this 21st century is a throw-away society and we tend to buy clothes as cheaply as we can get away with, pass them down to the charity shops and buy more.

So how do you play it? If we love the Lord and truly want the best for him we will want to be the best ourselves. At one time I was a Christian who was mean on myself, so that I could save money to give to God. Yes, I'm still thrifty, and perhaps that's due in part to the legacy from my childhood when I saw my mother making rag rugs from worn-out clothing, and even making things out of parachute silk, an acid yellowy green it was.

Now I try and get what I think are lovely and the right price, although I often make mistakes. One plan I put into action when I can, is to visit the better stores and look for the REDUCED racks. It's interesting that I have a couple of garments that really suit me well from five years ago and I still love wearing them. These were a red fairly-fitted warm top and another red and patterned top with a floppy neck line. They were sales lines from an expensive place.

So my tip would be that if it's finance that governs the clothes you wear, buy infrequently and well at sale prices.

Keep clothes for dirty work

Also, if you are at home and doing the housework and in the garden, don't just wear your good clothes all the time. I keep 'gardening clothes' - that's the stage in between what I consider just about worth wearing, and taking to the tip - in a bin near the back door. For me, they also serve as clothes to paint in. Oil paint does tend to get everywhere and you need white spirit to get it off.

In my mother's days there'd be those cotton wrap-over 'pinnies'. I remember that she would do all her housework in the morning, and then light the (real) fire(s) for the afternoon and evening, and after a post-lunch nap would change clothes. Unless you have a cleaner and a gardener, and all your hobbies are light and clean, have a set of clothes you can get mud and paint on quite happily. Then of course, if you find you are wearing nothing else, then it's time to liven up your life!

Hair

What about hair?

Now I really think this is important. If you feel good about your hair, you feel good, even if you are slouching around in slippers and an old jumpsuit. Someone's first impression of you is usually of your face, which is framed by your hair. I myself like a more natural look than the set coiffure that has been sprayed so hard it looks like a meringue, but ladies, even if it is getting thin on top, let's get professional advice, and enjoy looking as good as we can.

I have heard that there are mature Christian couples who save money by cutting each other's hair. Yes, it's adequate, but oh dear they would probably look much better groomed if occasionally they received the professional touch.

Every year I do an overview of my finances. I am horrified by what I spend on certain things, including hair, but I still stick by this premise, that it is really important.

Your face and body

We've considered clothes and hair. What about the body? Now I've dealt with exercise elsewhere, but if you are a rich Christian, and let's face it, there must be quite a lot of them, are you going to go the Botox route? I think even Joyce Meyer and Cliff Richard have tried it! This involves a small amount of poison temporarily paralysing part of you!

For me there is a dividing line between physically changing your body or skin and making it look good through what you apply or what you eat.

I pick up tips wherever I find them, and here's one I'd never heard of before. This woman was in her 80's and 90's and had the youngest looking face imaginable. She ran 15 minute sessions, as I understand it, charging £200, in what you could call 'face gymnastics'. What she did was to stretch her facial skin in different poses: grimaces, frowns, yells, rolling her lips, etc. holding them there a short while... and generally making the skin used to being pliable, so that it didn't automatically relax into the same grooves in old age.

I do this now, although not religiously, and I laugh when I think I ought to have started it years ago, but you could try. It's also a scheme only for those who live alone!

We can celebrate later life; we can celebrate older age. We don't have to be ashamed of a face that's had 60, 70 or 80 years of living. Beauty is in a face that is living; that shows emotions; that smiles. Beauty is not whether you look a carbon copy of a younger model.

So much of what we can do is free. Now I know some people for whom heaven is having sessions at a spa, being pampered, whether it's the ridiculous hot stones or being covered with mud. I know that they like it. I don't. I don't even like being massaged very much. Actually I can massage other people. My mother almost used to purr with pleasure when I massaged her ankles, and when I massaged her neck, a lot of her stress would just roll away.

You can of course, massage yourself. I happen to have particularly long arms so it's not hard to give my shoulders, legs and arms the 'once-over'.

I was once given a token for a beauty treatment. I looked at all the possibilities and decided on a body massage, and didn't enjoy that very much. As to lying there having your face pushed around and creamed etc.- no, it's not my scene. I'd get bored I think, if I couldn't talk to the beautician, get to know her and lead the conversation on to talking about Jesus.

However, I do recognise that regular massage of my face could help smooth it along. So every day when I put on the cream I spend a little time massaging. It's free. It's how I want it to be done. Let's take some of these so-called beauty treatments out of the hands of the professionals and do it ourselves.

The health of your body

This chapter is about staying and looking young.

We have considered the accoutrements that we put with our body. We've considered massage, but there is now the big issue of keeping your body really fit, not only keeping it the right size, but every organ of it being as whole as it can be. If you want to look good, you want to stay well.

This actually needs to be a project that we start in middle age. You can't suddenly realise you are overweight, have varicose veins and legs that get swollen and then suddenly become whole overnight. I always wonder how the unfortunate people, who are extremely obese, let themselves get to that state. To put it bluntly, each one of us can abuse our bodies by lack of exercise and incorrect diet.

There is growing evidence that if you are overweight you are more likely to develop health problems, such as heart disease, stroke, diabetes, certain types of cancer, gout (joint pain caused by excess uric acid), and gall bladder disease. Being overweight can also cause problems such as sleep apnoea (interrupted breathing during sleep) and osteoarthritis (wearing away of the joints); and the more overweight you are, the more likely you are to have these health problems.

Exercise

Now how can we, in later life, get enough exercise so that we can avoid a lot of illnesses that attack the elderly?

There are so many ways to do this. You may be a swimmer. My sister goes regularly to her local baths at a certain early morning time when it is free for senior citizens. She swims her thirty lengths but I think she enjoys even more the social side of swimming. She's got to know the regulars and it's like a little club.

Others of you may do vigorous gardening, mowing the lawn, cutting the hedges. You may belong to a rambling club, or even a speed-walking group. I tried that once, just once! You might do the school run on foot, walking to take your grandchildren to school and meeting them afterwards.

I am not going to say that you have to do exercise in only one way. However, I must share the means of exercise that I have done for about seven years, and I'm still excited about it and its effect.

I do my exercise at home. Probably seven years ago for my birthday I treated myself to a 'rebounder'. You probably haven't heard of one. Well, it looks like a mini trampoline but the surface is much harder. It is meant to be used inside, and you won't hit your head on your lounge ceiling if you jump on it. I often laugh to myself and wish I could introduce people to Jesus as effectively as I can introduce them to my rebounder. If I could, I'd have my own church of new converts by now!

The rebounder comes with instructions, ideas and warnings. It tells you not to use it for more than one and a half minutes at once, as its strong stuff! What - just jumping up and down? Well, you stand on it to start with and just get it moving. That's called therapeutic bouncing and it's really very pleasant. Apparently as you come out of gravity minutely, and the body throbs, you are bouncing out the lymph which is the bad stuff that you don't want in your body. My bouncer and I have come a long way together. I have bounced my way gently out of leg and hip aches; I have speeded up my recovery from a frozen shoulder and I regularly use it to stop colds, by extra bouncing to get the symptoms out. Then there's another advantage. If you wake up at 3:00 or 4:00 in the morning and can't seem to get back to sleep, you just need to bounce for a couple minutes and you've guaranteed yourself an immediate sleep before you know it. After I've tumbled back into bed to hug my hot water bottle once more, the two minutes bouncing always gives me an extra hour of sleep as minimum.

I now do about a quarter of an hour in the morning – to Christian music on CD - immediately after I get up. I don't just stand and jump on it but do all sort of exercises, for strengthening my stomach muscles, sitting back on my haunches, stretching, bending , anything I can manage. Then before my midday meal and my evening meal I do five minutes. It's not a hard task, as I enjoy watching television at the same time. I reckon that every doctor ought to recommend it to every patient. It does not claim to cure anything, but just to keep you so healthy that various ailments don't touch you.

I saw it for sale in a large store of high reputation. "Why don't people buy more of them?" I asked. "Because it's too simple," was the response. "People don't believe in them."

Oh yes, and I must also add that I have dropped a dress size through using it. I also picked up a tip on the telly. As you read this book you'll discover that I'm always picking up other people's tips. The theory presented to us was that to keep your body really healthy instead of twenty minutes of reasonable regular exercise, you just needed a very short amount of extreme exercise.

Now hold it! Whenever I hear that word 'extreme', I tend to be cautious. I know my body by now. You know yours. It means that when cutting the hedge I do twenty minutes at a time or else my shoulders ache. It means that when I'm on an intense musical theatre course I do not play their rough games.

However, the extreme exercise recommended was just running hard for thirty seconds, stopping for thirty seconds, then running again, in total for four minutes. The guinea pig and his control, running twenty minutes of easy exercise a week, were monitored and compared. The conclusion reached was that the short extreme exercise made for the healthier body and kept the blood pressure at the right level.

There's a tip, so at the end of my exercise I interpret my extreme exercise as just jumping from up high to crouching low a lot of times. I started at thirty, and now nine months on, I can do sixty jumps, which leaves me slightly out of breath. That is the simple recipe for me for feeling good and losing weight. Hurray!

If you exercise just before a meal, especially if you finish it with a minute's extreme exercise, you just don't want to each as much.

I don't think my friends actually believe me, when I say that I still enjoy chocolates after a meal and lovely desserts, but this routine does require discipline to do it three times a day, every day of your life! Just think though, you can lose a stone through just half an hour exercise a day!

Easy moving looks youthful

Your age is not only shown in your looks but how adept you are at moving. If you can move well you just don't look old. Another tip is this. I have found that walking up stairs is a chore in that your body weight has to rise up and fall on every stair. However, if you kind of make one movement of it, and glide, or run up the stairs, it is much easier. (Although don't show off to friends and end up with a bashed knee, and two osteopath appointments, like I did.)

I also make this little rule for myself, that unless it would be rude when I'm with a friend or in a group, I always climb up stairs and don't use the lifts, even up escalators in the tube, (maybe not the Northern line - that is a bit steep!).

Perhaps I'm helped by the fact that although I tried to get my home 'office' all together, I do enjoy sitting downstairs at a table by my lounge window, looking out on all who may visit me, while the computer is upstairs in my recording studio along with all my filing. So I'm often running up and down stairs. As I hear quoted, so often, 'Use it, but don't abuse it' and 'use it or you lose it'.

And what is glorifying to God in what I do or spend to stay looking good?

Someone said that the quick rule on finance was – spend some, save some, give some away. Get the balance right.

There is a later chapter on saving money and giving it away, and I touch on the subject in managing well, but keep your heart listening to God, and then I believe you'll spend the right amount on dressing that lovely person - which is you. When I browse round the stores at sale time, I have one sense which is trying to feel God's thought and another which has my current wardrobe in mind, and usually something my heart reaches out to is right, though I often make mistakes.

I think I almost dress better now than I did when my husband was alive. I am conscious of wanting to enjoy life and to show others I enjoy life.

8

Manage Well

Not everyone is a gifted manager, but the skill can be acquired and I think to live a successful, fruitful, satisfying life you must learn to manage yourself and your circumstances and for this you need wisdom and experience.

There are a lot of exhortations to obtain wisdom, in the Bible, "If any of you lack wisdom, you should pray to God, who will give it to you, because God gives generously and graciously to all." (James chapter 1 verse 5)

Chapters 8 and 9 of the book of Proverbs take wisdom as their main theme. For example: "Are you immature? Learn to be mature. Are you foolish? Learn to have sense." (Proverbs 8:5).

Wisdom is personified, and some commentators say that you could substitute the name Jesus for wisdom. Ask for wisdom.

What are the areas that you and I, in our later life, will need to manage? We could look at a few broad inclusive areas: home, time, money and relationships.

Management of the home

In your home, you need to keep on top of the utility bills, the council tax, and all the regular services that you pay for. We've all known this as a wife, mother or single person, and being in your later life is no excuse for not managing. A lot of payments may now be made on line. If this terrifies you there are the usual alternatives, but there is always someone to ring to help you.

Your house and garden need upkeep. You have to attend to smaller matters from replacing light bulbs, mowing the lawn, and getting the windows cleaned, to re-decoration when necessary, repair of fences, and replacing your fridge or computer. Can you put your hands on your receipt for the television that now has a part that won't work, and you think it should still be under guarantee?

Checking on utility meters

It's a good idea to check all your meters.

Nowadays you are always offered an on-line service. It usually saves a small percentage of the bill. Take control yourself, and check your meters monthly as then you can see if you are overdoing your usage.

Do you have a water meter? Mine is in the front garden next to the hedge. Well, just recently a really nice lady from the water board rang me to tell me that my bill this time was much larger than usual and was there a reason? Well, I pride myself on being economical with my water. This year I had decided to flush the toilet after two uses, if all is liquid. So it was a surprise and I first thought that the meter must be at fault.

When the man came round he discovered that the little dial on the meter was going round constantly and I showed him around the house that no water was being used. So that could mean a leak! Unbeknown to me, water had probably been leaking out somewhere in the garden for 6 months, and instead of paying me back £78, which I saw from the bill they were going to do, they were going to charge me £138! The process of getting the leak checked and repaired was too convoluted to be told here, but suffice to say that it took from mid August to mid December to get it totally sorted.

If I had known about the possibility of leaks, I would have checked it every month. Why did they not warn their customers? Manage well!

Finding things when you need them

I tell you, most of the frustration in life is not being able to find things when they are needed.

Yes we keep them, but how ordered are your files? I still use paper and a proper metal filing cabinet. You might use boxes, or even go electronic, and keep every detail on the computer, but a regular check of where everything is brings much comfort. Often through the year there is no call to delve into that particular drawer, or that box, but it's such a good idea to do so regularly. (I speak to myself here!) You might have put away some Christmas presents, having seen just the right thing for your cousin or your friend at a craft fair in March, and put them away in a safe place but now can't find them. Check regularly. Re-ordering your bookshelves is also a good, if time–consuming, task. Can any books actually go to the charity shop?

Such a lot of unasked-for paper comes through my door. There's the Indian take-away, the pizza delivery, the charity appeals, the solar heating promotions and the latest Saga holiday brochures. Sometimes I think that I ought to consider one in detail, so I leave it aside in a sub-pile to be considered later. That is a mistake! The stuff accumulates and often hides something really important that I need to get my hands on. What I should do is to discipline myself to check through the junk mail and deal with it straight away. Then I'd have a lot less clutter.

My first job after school before I went to university was as a library assistant in Birmingham. Before that I was a fairly 'arty' young person, but I soon realised that without order in a library nothing can happen, whether 'shelving' those books, carrying a tower of books along the stack and putting them back in author order, or checking in the books - yes it was the 'brown card' system then. Computers hadn't invaded the scene at that time. I realised then the power and even the reassurance of order.

Manage each day

Particularly if you are now at home a lot of the time, you need to manage the pattern of your day. Yes it's back to rhythm again.

Now in later life we usually have more spare time to manage. This can be a glorious advantage. It can be a problem. Let's think of the pluses. Not many of us will be rushing out of the door at a very early hour, having bolted breakfast, to catch a train to work. We won't usually be trying to get the children out of bed and through their breakfast with their bag packed for school, unless we are doing what more and more grandparents are doing. So, most of us have an early morning without much interruption. This is a blessing! I don't know many people over 70 who 'sleep on' a lot, but we can surely relax into a good early morning routine. We have the privilege of setting the scene of the day with our Maker. ' I may be checking and doing emails between 8:00 and 9:00 but that follows a really relaxed time with God, as there is no pressure. What a bonus.

Now everyone has a 'to do' list, but variety helps the day along enormously. So if you have the following on your list, (check and answer emails, ring up friend, make the dentist appointment, cut the hedge in the back garden, de-frost the freezer, start a new painting, choose music for your Christian programme), what order would you put them in?

That list is geared especially to me, but I think we wouldn't put the dentist, the hedge and de-frosting the freezer first, would we? Human nature is such that we leave the hardest things till last and possibly don't do them at all.

Here's an idea! Go for change and variety. Put a session at the computer next to cutting the hedge. Then sit down again to do a painting and then de-frost the fridge. I'm not a specialist by nature. I have a flight of fancy that if I stuck at something for four hours a day (e.g. piano playing) I would be brilliant, but you see I could never stick at it as I don't have the stamina or patience. Look at your make-up and plan accordingly. While I am writing this book I plan to go and do something very physical next. More than an hour or so on a computer is quite enough for me at any given time.

Always do the difficult things first.

Back to my 'to do' list. Nothing can beat the satisfaction of crossing out each item. When I feel weak, I don't just put CLEAN THE HOUSE, but CLEAN THE KITCHEN, CLEAN THE UTILITY, CLEAN THE BATHROOM etc which means I can get even more satisfaction from crossing off the task from that list.

Comparing this rather sad little stratagem with others, I find that we all do it.

However, do you find that certain items have to be forwarded from day to day? My guess is that these will be the difficult ones. Come on now, you 'ladies of later life', you must try and do the difficult ones first, and I speak to myself too.

There's also the case for doing necessary small jobs immediately you discover them. I'm thinking of the toilet roll on its last two leaves, or the batteries wearing out on the electric toothbrush. I also find that if I'm not sure of what to do about an email it is dangerous to leave it untouched, as the type goes from bold to regular and it is forgotten. Maybe that's why some very respected people, even clergy, never answer my emails!

Manage your money well

Do you ever think about what you spend? It's a taxing exercise if you are honest. I would urge you to know how far your money is going. Do an overview of where you finance goes in details each year. You'll be surprised how much even the most economical of us spend on food.

Here are some ideas of headings:

- Business expenses
- Pension
- Giving - regular giving; one-off giving
- Council tax
- Utilities - water, electricity, gas
- Telephone - land line; mobile telephone
- TV licence
- Holidays
- House and garden
- Garden maintenance

- Cleaner (if you have one)
- House and contents insurance
- Car - petrol, service and MOT, repairs, insurance, road tax
- Assistance
- Personal
- Hair
- Clothing
- Leisure interests
- Food
- Gifts

This may take time to initiate, but there is a satisfaction of being in charge, under God, of what he has given us.

Check on the satisfaction levels of what you always do

I don't recommend changing suppliers of this and that all the time but be savvy about what's out there. Sometimes the hassle of a saving scheme is not worth the time you spend on it. When I was married I used to have a 'store card' until I realised that meant that when I had spent something, it hadn't actually gone immediately out of my account and there was a nasty surprise when it *was* taken out a month later!

If you like to have overseas holidays, but come home with great relief to your own house and garden, consider what price you put on that holiday. Was it worth it? Could you take bus trips and coach trips for days out or a weekend in Britain, with equal satisfaction? Do exactly what suits you, and be yourself, not comparing yourself to other people.

Manage your relationships well

Let's face it. If you are on your own as I am, you have to get used to initiating events to keep relationships going. People don't consciously cut you out, but many couples are sufficient in themselves, and forget, if they ever knew, what it is like to be on your own as your basic default programme. I find that very few of my single friends will contact me with the idea of a 'get together', but they are very happy for me to arrange it. There's no good moping. Enjoy giving yourself time to build up good relationships with those you know.

I personally find that history counts for a lot. I mean that the friends I was close to twenty or twenty five years ago are still precious to me, even if I don't see them often. We have so much common ground from the past, so that sharing the present is easy. On the other hand those relationships that you tend to make in a new church don't quite have the same depth, as time has not passed to weather and hone the jewel that is your friendship.

Neighbours

With neighbours, too, sometimes you have to pocket your pride and ring them up or pop round to them. Now I am quite reluctant to do this although at times I just long for a bit of human contact. Very precious to me was a period when I was working in radio full time, living in a small village, and after I had come home exhausted, turned on the grill, turned on the telly, fed the cat and come to myself, by about 9pm I would just wonder down a couple of doors to an older couple who were always in, and just spend half an hour chatting with them. Good neighbours willing to give time to you are worth their weight in gold.

Be wary, know yourself

In later life, we have to be careful about talking too much. We do tend to pour out all the things we have done and our frustrations and joys on someone else. I have noted that when single people arrive I sometimes get quite fed up at the time they take talking about themselves. Then I think, "Ah...you live alone... and I understand." To manage a relationship well we must be really generous. I know a lovely man and his wife down in Bournemouth. He has the knack of drawing everything out of you without you noticing. He gives nothing much away about himself but just listens and listens to you. We could all learn from that. In relationships we must get back to Jesus' principle of thinking of the other person first. Indeed, of thinking of that person as better than ourselves. It is possible to become quite selfish in later life.

One way to honour others and to make them feel good is to remember their birthdays. At the start of the year, I put everyone's birthday down in my diary. A well chosen card and thought means such a lot to people. You have remembered them.

Manage your relationships, build them up, but keep a right balance. We have to be wary of someone else subtly taking control over us, when we are aiming to serve them. The other day I heard a talk comparing people to radiators and drainers. Radiators bring warmth to any situation. The speaker talked of rushing into the supermarket for a quick shop but seeing with dread someone she knew would be a 'drainer'.

On the other hand though, usually the more we put in, the more we get out, and as Jesus put us on this earth to serve, a right relationship should be a real joy to us.

Meeting a possible spouse

There is, of course, always the possibility of meeting your next husband or wife in later life. Because I have been on my own for ten years, I have got a very creative pattern of broadcasting, painting, writing and doing Christian voluntary work in schools, so I don't know how a new man in my life would work out. It would be very exciting if God set it up. I just heard today of a man called Paddy, aged 90, marrying a lady of 92 and having a proper wedding!

What I would actually like more, I think, would be a few really good men friends, who would ring up and say "Elspeth can you do next Tuesday? I'll pick you up at 5:30... we're going for an early meal and then the theatre. Everything's booked." What bliss not to have to organise your own entertainment or transport or parking. However, we can't always have what we want. I think if more mature men knew that not all women are looking to grab the whole of them and devour them in a marriage, but would like a little of their company here and there, they'd be braver to ask us out!

Manage your responses – yes or no

As a single person in later life, but still highly able, you may be asked to do so many things, particularly as you are probably not working, or not working full time. Don't say 'yes' immediately to anything. Consider well, mull it over. Will this thing enhance your life as well as helping others or will it be a drag for you? Only you can get the balance right.

Managing new communication

I am not a natural on the computer. I've heard it said that it's the curious who get adept at computer skills very quickly. Now I am not curious. I once had a gas cooker with a compartment at the base with all sorts of add-on extras and gismos. I must confess that a year later, I think I hadn't even tried one of them. On a computer, I need great courage to press keys without being sure what they do. "I could delete everything," I panic to myself.

However, the advantages of the internet today to those of us in later life can hardly be exaggerated. Take emails which some of us take for granted. Think how quickly we can communicate to anyone anywhere, and as we are probably spending more time in our homes than out, what a life-line to friends!

Then there's the whole world to discover. You can explore a village in Britain as though you were there, you can find a recipe for carrot cake, you can track down your ancestors, you can hone your bridge playing so that your narrow world enlarges a thousandfold. It's probably not always a good thing to look up your ailments though. You might think you had a terminal disease when all you had was something like a nettle rash!

If you are terrified of starting on a computer, you have a thousand people who feel the same. You are not alone. However these thousands are starting to go on computer courses run by bodies concerned with the over 60's in every town. I have been using the computer for many years now, but I still phone a friend sometimes, to ask whether to right click or left click

Go on, put in the work to manage new technology, and you will reap great rewards of satisfaction. I suppose I ought then to encourage you to use iPhones with apps that do everything, and ipads, like David Hockney does, to create colourful drawings, but I have yet to move in that direction. However, I could have twenty years or more to grace this earth so you never know! More later.

9

Control Your Mind

Think about your mind. It is the most complicated internet system in the world and it's all in you. If you could 'google' every facet of your past and present thoughts, the possibilities would be infinite. As a test of your memory, take yourself back to your childhood and a favourite place, maybe your own bedroom, maybe your gran's house. I know there are places where I can take my inner torch and shine it on every detail. In my grandparents' house was a pantry, or larder. You had to go down steps to it, stone steps, and there were raised concrete areas all around on which lay the various dishes. But what was terrifying to me was that in the ceiling were hooks, and from the hooks dangled dead birds, destined for the pot!

You must have vivid memories too! What place can you bring alive? You might even have been jotting down enjoyable memories from the past.

Imagination

If I asked you to imagine a scenario, say for a story, you would be able to do it easily. You might set your story in a Cornish village, where an artist languished in a rented room, unkempt, under-nourished as he wasn't a very good artist. He would often wander to the pub where he fancied the barmaid that was on at weekends, but the relationship never got anywhere.

Your story would be unique as you can imagine just exactly what you want to. It's your mind enjoying playing games with the multi-million thoughts that can be brought to the surface like grains of sand on the sea shore.

Various inputs

You can add to your mind's memory store all the time. Some of the additions are subconscious, for instance that sunset over the sea with your grandchildren silhouetted in black against it. You don't consciously press the add button to get the sunset. Of course some of the additions you really need to work at. For instance, mastering the words of that poem you want to recite at a friend's ruby wedding or recalling people' names.

The interplay of one thought upon another, the mix, the comparisons, the layers of thought on the same subject are highly complicated. There are all sorts of different 'inputs' into your mind.

There's the visual input, like people you see on the bus, the audible input, like the cries of your grandchild who won't go to sleep, the sensory input, like the whiffs of a certain perfume. I remember, with delight, the smell of a certain glue. I found it delightful because it brought back memories of my daddy mending something of mine when I was very little. There are also feelings: feelings of anxiety about a loved one and much more. All these inputs are fed into that amazing part of us we call 'the mind'.

As we move into later life, we can live in the past. Our minds can run the film back to our very earliest days. For some very old friends the only things that make them come alive are good memories. If you have a whole lifetime of good memories, that is great, but to stay there for too long means we are not being fulfilled in the present. We can, as it were, take down a memory off the shelf and enjoy it and put it back again. For those of us who are bereft of a husband, wife, mother, daughter, there is a sweet delight in remembering the best moments, the best words, the loveliest scenes. Don't be afraid to enjoy not just today's you, but the 'you' of the past.

Bad memories

However, mixed alongside the good memories are sad memories, bad memories and memories of embarrassing moments! All sorts of things can creep into our consciousness unbidden, and give us real grief. Putting it down here brings it back to mind but for a long time when I heard a programme which said that some unscrupulous dealers, when discovered by a farmer, retaliated by going and cutting the legs off his dog. Well, I couldn't get rid of that tortuous memory for a long time. It still hurts as I write this.

Good news

However, for the Christian, there is good news. We ourselves are in control of our minds. We don't have to ask Jesus for the gift of disciplining our minds, of bringing them into order. God says he is transforming our minds, if we are believers. We ourselves have authority in Jesus over our own minds. Anyone can be tempted, but they don't have to sin. You can fleetingly entertain a thought that isn't helpful, but then you can refuse to think of it again, and put other thoughts in its place. Joyce Meyer in her book, 'Battlefield of the Mind', deals extensively with this.

I really think we can move more into the realm of believing in this transformation. Think about it. It's written in the Bible in the present tense: Romans 12:2. It doesn't say, 'God HAS transformed your mind'. He IS transforming it. This is a process and I'm sure the gradual transformation will happen only as we stay very close to the person of Jesus letting his words ring in our ears constantly, and letting his Spirit guide us and help us.

Times of day

Let's get more specific. When you wake up in the morning what state of mind are you in? Maybe you're feeling rough because of bad dreams or maybe your mind is just a blank page at that time. I usually work out which day of the week it is to start with and then I have a framework to think through. I have taken on a habit of actually saying, "Good Morning" to Jesus, the Father and the Holy Spirit, as I want them in on the very beginning of my day. I do a brief confession of any sin that may have eluded me, then often put on the armour of God (from that so well-used passage in Ephesians 6). Then my mind gets going on the duties and delights of the day.

Bad thoughts - three types

There are probably three main sorts of bad thoughts. The first sort involves bad thoughts that come up in a mind unbidden which concern what is happening at the moment, not from what has happened in the past. These concern our reaction to others, quite often pride. We may, in some way, be glad that we are not like that other person; oh yes, just like the Pharisee and the publican in the temple. Or we might be on the phone, saying pleasing words, but wishing our caller would get off the line as we are in the middle of a good programme on TV and are not recording it and so will miss it unless we bother to sort out the play-back alternatives!

For these thoughts we need to respond quickly with repentance and then clear our minds to think a few positive thoughts in their place.

The second type of bad thoughts are those which come up concerning things you have done or said in the past that you shouldn't have said or done. Perhaps you told your best friend about someone else's private confidence, and then realised with dismay - too late - what you've done. Maybe something comes up from the past, like when you hurt your mother and you glimpsed some tears there, and you wished you'd kept your tongue.

These are obviously thoughts of self condemnation. Wonderfully in Jesus, we can be quickly clear of these thoughts. We are forgiven by his death on the cross for the state of sin we are in, and "if we confess our sin he is faithful and just to forgive us our sins," (I John 1:9). So we can quickly clear these away, and know we are washed white as snow.

Then there's a third type of unhelpful, bad thoughts. These come to us through something we have seen or heard or read, that make us fear or feel repulsion. Paul said to think on those things that are pure holy and true. I have interesting debates with a lovely Baptist minister, born again, and evangelistic, who is really keen on horror films. He must be the exception. I do think for most of us, that to allow evil to pop into our minds and rest there, is not helpful to living a holy life. Peter, in his first letter,

(1:16), quoted a verse from Leviticus (11:44), God saying, "Be holy, as I am holy."

Giovanni Payne, in a talk on how to get through difficult times, said, "Don't let your mind be a waste bin for the devil."

If we limit the amount of evil our eyes, ears and consciousness take in, then it will be easier to control our thoughts, and to enjoy later life.

Sometimes our minds are full of mundane thoughts that can be depressing. I wonder if these can be transformed by the control of our mind. Thinking about my lifestyle and things I wasn't keen on, I realised that I don't really like putting petrol in the car or washing my hair. Then I thought, perhaps I could change that. So I actually thanked God for the business of washing my hair and tried to dispel the chore aspect of it.

So I believe we can choose what we think about. We have control of our minds. We don't need to know the bad things about other people and gossip about it. We don't need to harbour thoughts that come in and do us no good. God is transforming our minds. I believe he can actually wipe out bad memories.

Prepare yourself at bedtime if you get troubled thoughts in the night, especially in that later more shallow sleep, after maybe you've woken up and gone back to sleep again. Firstly, before you switch off the radio, turn off the light, and wriggle into your most comfortable position, invite the Holy Spirit to take over your mind while you are asleep. Remember Christ's death and ask that his blood covers you. Ask the Father's protection of your mind, as you can't control it while you are asleep. Happily, God 'neither slumbers nor sleeps.'

Your mind contains as many thoughts and images as there are drops of water in the ocean. It's a neutral medium that can be tarnished with rubbish and evil or it can glow with right and positive godliness. You can enjoy your imagination, you can enjoy your past history and you can enjoy the present. To keep your mind clean in God's sight, make him the curator of your store of past and present thoughts.

Give yourself a challenge - mentally and creatively

It is also necessary, as you get older, to keep your mind as keen and sharp as you can. Why shouldn't you write a poem, cook a complicated dish, start drawing even if you think you're so bad that you never show your work to people.

Last summer I booked onto a musical theatre holiday in Scarborough. It sounded good. We were to work at and perform an adapted, shortened version of the Gilbert and Sullivan operetta, 'Iolanthe'. I had been to musical holidays in the past, but had found them very taxing as there was an enormous amount of material to be learned then and there, and memory is not my strongest thing.

I went up by train and was delighted to find God had sent me an angel to negotiate the change at York and find our bus in Scarborough. Sitting at my reserved table seat I saw that the young man opposite was reading through a vocal score. My spirits rose, and yes, on enquiry, he was going to exactly the same place as I was.

However, I hadn't realised that being on my own and new would be so difficult. Almost everyone there had been before, during the previous year. There was the problem of finding my way around and of keeping up mentally with various vocal and physical exercises. I had thought I'd audition for a part, but only realised when I got there that the whole school, about a hundred of them, watched all auditions. I was so nervous that I blew it, and made a real fool of myself I thought, (although I did get a small solo part).

It was a great comfort for me to have some Christian CD's to listen to in my room. It was a hard experience, especially mentally, but I hope I have grown because of it. It was certainly a challenge. I don't think I'd have gone if I'd known how much of a challenge it would be. God knew, and allowed me to be his representative there.

Other mental challenges present themselves almost weekly to me. Most organisations including my church rely on us continually checking their websites. Sometimes I could scream when asked for yet another password. Yet I know that I must do this thing.

So what could be your mental challenge? Perhaps you are a 'sudoko' expert or a crossword guru. Work out what stretches you and don't shy away from it. This part of later life sometimes requires hard work, but it's a common saying,

"If you don't use it, you'll lose it."

10

Eliminate Potential Stress

Are you prone to get nervous about things? Maybe you sail through life trusting that everything is always going right, but I do find that stress is a trick of the devil that I do not want, and I need to work on its elimination.

I appreciate that there is good stress, which gets a job done. Most of us work better with a dead-line. Have you ever tried to learn anything new on your own, without a teacher or mentor? Once I tried to learn the tenor recorder and set myself a daily time to practise. But the flesh is weak, and there was no lesson at the end of the week, no teacher to reprimand or encourage, so the recorder got left behind. Good stress moves you to achieve a goal, and this was missing.

Many people go to 'Weight Watchers' to lose weight because they have to announce their weight when they arrive in public. There is this pressure to eat less or have more exercise so that they will not be shamed before others. Often when you are suddenly asked to, say, write an article, or complete a task, the necessary deadline gives you motivation.

On the other hand, we are all very much aware of the negative stress, because it affects our bodies as well as our minds. This usually takes the form of muscular pain in the back. My mother would get me to massage her neck and her ankles. I didn't know what brought that much stress on her - perhaps I should have communicated more, but for myself I know the stress of, for instance, 'can't cope-itis', (that's what I call it) where the list of difficult things to do makes you numb and feeling totally inadequate to do anything.

So my thought is this. Work out ways to avoid getting into a place where stress might happen. You may say that it's easier said than done, but you can put certain contingency plans into action.

Also, another tip from Geo Payne was to prepare beforehand for difficult situations. Be armed with quotes from the Bible. Be ready for the moments when you know you are going to 'lose it'. When it says we are 'more than conquerors', it means, that before we've faced the battle, we have won.

Parking

I don't find parking easy. People say that women have little 'spacial' awareness, and I think I agree with them. It's not a crime, it's not a sin, it's how we are made! I have been parking for umpteen years and still get in and out of the car several times to check its position. I still leave about six feet too much room. Sorry women, I mustn't lump all my sex together as having the same weakness. It was fine when my husband was alive. Getting to shops in the centre was a matter of being dropped off and meeting him later at a pre-arranged place and time, preferably for a coffee.

Right, so parking is difficult for me. That means that arriving when most of the spaces are taken is stressful. I might have to squeeze myself into an almost impossibly small space or I might have to scour the area for other roads to park in, or work out the instructions on an expensive public car park with discs and machines and, worse still, tall concrete columns that just ask to be scraped!

So what is the obvious course? My plan is to travel ten or fifteen minutes earlier than required when I know that parking will be difficult. This means that I am sure to find a space and I don't get any stress. That's just one example of not letting myself get in a stressful situation.

My friend has just discovered 'Park and Ride' schemes. My first thought was that they are expensive, but then, in later years, we all have a free bus pass so it could be the answer to my parking problems but only in the cities that use this scheme.

Yes, free buses are a boon, but you have to be someone who has lots of time. I'm afraid my life is packed full and I can't always afford the time to wait at a bus stop when the bus might come in two minutes or in twenty, and then of course, we all know they come in threes!

Holiday travel

Now connected with parking is another area of stress but one we can well plan for and eliminate. If you are flying from an airport, my advice is to choose a flight that does not start at 6 or 7 or 8 in the morning. It might be cheaper. It might give you nearly another day there, but as you usually have to check in 2 hours before, just think what time you are going to get up in the morning. I know from experience that if you need to get up at 4:00am, even if you have your trusty alarm set correctly, you will wake at 1:00 and at 2:00 and at 3:00, which makes you feel like a wreck for the first day of your holiday. Alternately you need to spend a night in a local B&B or hotel. Oh, it just isn't worth it! Yes, your 11am flight might cost a bit more, but it will take so much tension out of the whole event.

And another thing - choose the airport you find most congenial. As I live in St.Albans I know that on the weekdays there is a through train to Gatwick, which takes you right into the check - in area. What could be better! Time has long passed when the adventure was worth any sacrifice!

Then there's the stress of being nervous

I belong to an operatic society. I am usually a strong voice in the chorus, but occasionally I audition for principal parts, and then my nervousness stops my voice from behaving as it should. Once I auditioned for the part of a housekeeper in the 'Man of le Mancha' - the story of Don Quixote, as told by its author in prison. (You know, he's the partially mad knight who tilted at windmills). There were only fifteen people in this production sharing parts and all of us would be on the stage all the time. As usual, at my audition I sang abysmally because of nerves so I thought that of course I hadn't got the part. However, I received a phone call from the director to ask me to come and try again as she knew- well it was obvious - that I was nervous.

So this time, I was not going to let the stress get in my way. I was leading pre-school music groups at the time, so I made them listen for three minutes, whether I or they were embarrassed or not, so that I could practise before an audience. And indeed I got the part and happily played an aristocratic prisoner, a housekeeper and a donkey at different times in the play.

Computers

If we are to live successfully in this century, we have to have a certain modicum of computer skills. Let's face it, unless you hide under the false cloak of old age, you need to be part of modern communication. You really need to be able to write emails and respond. Oh how much easier communication has become when to send a message overseas you don't have to buy a thin folded piece of blue paper – an airmail letter - and take it to the post office. Do you remember that? It used to take weeks to get there. Now you can tap out a message and it arrives instantly.

There are a lot of add -on skills of course, and it is so useful to type down thoughts or Christmas lists or whatever. However, when people start sending you photographs and other attachments, and you want to send some back, which requires a digital camera and popping that tiny little miniature chocolate biscuit of a memory card into the printer, yes, I admit, things do get complicated.

Now for some, you may have just the mind that enjoys this challenge. You are curious by nature and are happy to explore the machine without fear of deleting everything. You are a 'silver surfer' in your element. You have grasped the market place called 'ebay' and can shop online every hour, given the chance.

But I'm afraid I stand with those who are still asking at times, "Right click or left click?"

Just lately I have felt really on the edge of stress when the time taken to upload a programme I broadcast, doubled. Each week I need to send a programme to the Radio Verulam computer. Normally, if I click on the right places and put in the correct letters, it uploads a fifty-five minute programme in twenty minutes. However, in the last fortnight it has taken forty five minutes, and sometimes has started to back track on itself and then made that nasty sound, the 'uh-oh' which is its way of saying that it has failed to complete.

So I have been on to my provider 'Talktalk' for half an hour this morning. The chap with an Indian accent, was difficult to understand, and not very patient, but finally I agreed to running this test through the day. Now they want to send an engineer out.

This is stress! I am stalling, taking advice from the radio station engineer and a 'Talktalk' person, and needing to get my programme through, as no-one wants a radio with a blank space for two hours.

So what is my contingency plan? I think the main thing is to have dependable sources of real help. People say you have to pocket your pride to do this, but not me. I love help. Get Help! Learn what you can yourself but don't blame yourself for not knowing enough.

Entertaining

Do you get stress from entertaining, and cooking for others? I have an 85 year old neighbour. We met nearly ten years ago when we were both walking our dogs in the local vicinity. Discovering she was new to the area we chatted, and discovered we were both widows. So our friendship formed. Helen was trained in domestic science. She is an excellent cook. She would provide meals for six or eight when her JP husband brought back important people.

She has fed her three children and her grand-children round the table for many years. In fact she still enjoys cooking. It's a natural relaxation for her, so I must admit I order my homemade Christmas cake from her. She would never get stressed at cooking, until her 'forgettery' gets really bad.

For me, I am not in a cooking layer of life. There was a time when I would cook a Sunday lunch for twelve every Sunday, and we'd invite all the students who were around back to our house, whether there were five or fifteen. It was exhilarating! It gave them a bit of home comfort, and I even bought a set of white dinner plates at £2 a piece to go alongside the Minton set we had that would probably fetch £50 a piece now.

But now I haven't entertained folk for a meal for several years, and I would be utterly stressed in doing so. Therefore the contingency plan would be to ask each friend to bring a dish, or take them all out to a local restaurant.

You don't HAVE to be stressed, and I say that to myself as much as to anyone

Forgetting where you put things

Do you often go upstairs or into another room, and then wonder what you went there for? I put that down to lack of focus on the immediate thing. And lack of focus can also cause the most miniscule of stress points that can be so irritating. You forget where you put things.

Now with the help of an old metal filing cabinet, which I rearranged with headings in alphabetical order only last year, and with my household arranged so that everything has its place, I should be able to keep good order. However, I am on my way from the bedroom, with my 'to do' list in my hand, but on the way down to the lounge I pop a dirty coffee cup in the kitchen sink. Then I settle down on the settee and see which TO DO thing I am going to do first... and the list is not there. Back up to the bedroom? No it's not there, but while I'm up there I take the dirty clothes basket down to the utility to start the washing. Now what was it I lost? The clue should be in the last place, which is the bedroom. No? It was the TO DO list, which, yes, must be in the kitchen but first I'll just go to the loo.

You see what I mean! But how do I cure myself of this malaise? Do I have to be a one-stop person? It's so natural to carry out about three little tasks at the same time. However, I suppose if this gets really stressful, one will have to get one little job at a time, and be prepared to run up and down stairs three times instead of once!

Forgetting names

An important skill that matters a lot in your social scene is remembering names. I believe that most of us, from about 50 upwards, suffer from this and it gets worse.

First there's the instant recollection that eludes us. You are introduced to someone in a group or individually. You repeat their name, but you are also drinking in the visual side of the information in front of you. Beryl has a sparkly necklace, fairly mauve lipstick and her hair is really short, and she is tall. I take that in but don't remember her name. My brain doesn't seem to handle too much input all at once. As I don't mind making a fool of myself, if I forget the name within five or ten minutes of chatting, I do ask again, but unless I make a joke of it, and talk about forgetting names, it might just waft out of my brain almost straight away.

Secondly, there's the blank in our mind when the name of a person we know well is just not there instantly. There's a dreadful blank, although from experience after waiting for a short time to elapse, our computer-type brains will dredge it from the lost bin.

One answer to this memory loss is to make a habit of browsing through your address book or your computer contacts list. I used to have five hundred pre-school children in thirty seven groups over the week, when I led music groups. I prided myself that I knew nearly all the children's names, although not their mothers' names. I could do this because in front of me, for each group, there was a page with their names in alphabetical order. I was continually reminding myself of the names through visual means - the words on paper - and I could match them with the real children.

I have discovered that if I take the time to glance through lists of my friends, family and contacts, then, when called upon, I can recall their name much more easily. I remember things by sight much more than through hearing things. I suppose we all learn in different ways. By now, I know myself quite well!

If it's a third type of memory loss, like you just can't think of the prime minister's name, or that celebrity who was in the news, that is a bit more to do with ageing, and I haven't an instant answer, except keeping your mind as alive as possible.

Forgetting can be stressful, and here are a few other quick points of possible stress.

Embarrassing mistakes

I think in my life that my embarrassing mistakes have been much greater burdens to me than my sins. I find it's hard to forgive myself, and to get over looking like a fool. The mistake does tend to linger in your mind. Joyce Meyer puts this down to pride. She might be right.

The most recent one was so funny, I've almost enjoyed it though it did hang heavy on me one night, so that I couldn't get to sleep.

I go to ballroom dancing classes on a Thursday night. It's an excellent set up. You don't need a partner and it's 'pay as you go' so if you don't like the jive, or if the rumba puts your hips out, or you have an unavoidable other commitment, then you don't lose out. Beginners start at 7:30, there's a quick break for a glass of water at 8:15 and then the slightly harder class starts. Then at 9:00 there's a real break for a cup of tea and goodies to eat. The organiser makes us banana bread at times, but there's fruit cake and nearly always those delicious chocolate fudge cakes.

On this one occasion I opted for the chocolate fudge cake, and being a warm night, and us being quite hot with dancing, my fingers got a bit 'chocolaty'. As I happened to be far away from my handbag with its helpful tissues, my fingers had to stay a bit chocolaty, but then a chap called Brian asked me to dance with him. You see, in the break there's free dancing, and often couples who come together take this chance to dance together, as all the rest of the evening they are passing from partner to partner. Well, I very happily went off to try the quickstep or whatever with him and forgot my fingers. However, to my horror, having done one dance with him, I looked at his shoulders. There were long brown chocolate finger marks on his white shirt. And here I must confess I was an utter coward. I didn't even mention it, and on the way home, opened my eyes in disbelief at what I'd done, but also roared with laughter.

That, actually, was the only funny embarrassing moment I've had, not to be compared with going into the men's loos in my stress before finals at Exeter university or forgetting the words that I had said successfully hundreds of times, in a musical theatre audition.

Brian was there the next week. I wondered if he'd either be too polite to say anything, or had tossed his shirt straight in the laundry basket without noticing the chocolate finger marks, or whether he'd tease me with it. I was prepared to confess all and grovel, but nothing was said!

So what takes the stress out of these embarrassing moments? I would advise that you share the incident with a friend. That friend will help you see that mistakes are not sins, and with a friend you can laugh, not cry! Happily I did do that with my embarrassing moment with Brian's white shirt.

Know your limits

One of my weaknesses, which I have come to know as a tolerated enemy in the camp, is my poor memory. Yes, I stretch it with crosswords, and games, and mental agility as far as I can, but I still need a 'sat nav' or maps if anywhere I go has more than three roundabouts for me to negotiate, until I've been there five times.

I feel that people look down on me for this and think that I'm lazy, or not trying, but, believe me, it is congenital in my case.

This poor memory is instanced in my piano playing. I teach piano to children and beginner adults. I still have about thirty five pupils a week, and I think I am probably a better teacher because I recognise that learning can be a slow process and I'm always thinking of different ways of getting the children to move forward in mastering the instrument. However I have worked out over the years that there are several different skills in playing the piano, and one person may have one or two or indeed all of them. I have the skill of sight reading. I can look at nearly any piece of music and play it reasonably on sight. Having accompanied for the musical Carousel, for my operatic society, I am sometimes called on as a reserve. One evening I was called in at an hour's notice to play for a rehearsal of South Pacific, and it happened that for the first time they were running the whole of the show. Whew! My shoulders ached when I got home. However, I managed to make a credible pass at it and was appreciated.

So I can sight read. Another skill of the pianist is to play pieces from memory. Apart from a few nursery rhymes which I played daily for pre-school music groups for twenty six years, I cannot play anything, not anything, from memory! My young pupils can do this much better than I can.

There is also the third skill and this is a real gift, to be able to play music you have heard, straight onto the piano.

But here I emphasise memory

I mentioned my ballroom dance class just a few pages back in talking of embarrassing moments. The first class is for beginners but anyone there takes part. This is happily taught really slowly. Then we continue and although the sequences in themselves stick in my memory, when the time comes to put them all together I might not remember. If I can get to this point remembering most steps I can eat my tea and cakes and go home happily.

There is another class afterwards, for those of intermediate level, but I haven't yet stayed to it. While I could perform really well, until my brain can remember the quick sequence of different steps, I don't feel confident to stay on. One day I shall feel totally confident after the dance at 9:00, but so far I don't. Not many of us leave at 9:00. Even those who've had less experience than I have stay on... but they don't have to work with a poor memory like mine, and believe you me, I do really concentrate.

I may be thought the less of, but my contingency plan is to leave while I feel good about what I do, and not to put myself in a position of being deflated by failing the challenge of the harder group.

Indeed it was the same in the adult tap class I used to attend. There were about twenty of us between ages of 17 and 70, and I was in my 50's. I managed to get to Bronze level... but I was the slowest in the class until just before the exam, and then I used to obtain some of the highest marks of the group, because I could perform well, when I'd actually learnt the sequences.

So I say, KNOW YOURSELF, and make provision for your own weaknesses, at the same time remembering that God made your shape and you have no need to be ashamed of how you are. I have to keep telling that to myself!

'Can't-cope-itis'

This really does bring on stress. You have taken on too much to do, you can't do it peaceably, but you have to do it, and you get all screwed up, and it really affects your body - usually with an aching back. The only advice I can give is: Don't take on too much. Always have that link with the Father. Is this okay ? Should I be doing this?

When you are asked to do something, even if it is right up your street and you feel a lift inside you, always say you'll think about it, before enthusiastically making promises.

Even if you are expected to do something, for example, putting up relations for the night, if your time schedule makes it impossible, you have to keep your sanity and say no.

Notes to yourself

Why not prepare for warfare against stress in all its forms, not only by reaching down and channelling the peace of God into yourself continually, but by listing possible stresses and contingency plans. For me it would go something like this:

1. Parking plan - ask someone where to park - go early - get a lift.
2. Might run out of petrol - plan - never let your tank reach the almost line.
3. Forgotten to turn things off - plan - always go round every single room and outside and do a quick check.
4. Can't face righting an embarrassing mistake - plan ring a close friend and get wisdom and sympathy.
5. Too much to do - 'can't-cope-itis' – plan - say 'no' more often.
6. Over the top hospitality - ought to house those relations who want to stay but can't cope - plan - say 'no'.
7. Forgetting where to put thing – plan - focus on one thing at a time.
8. Entertaining - plan - don't do what you haven't done for years - ask for contributions or go out to a meal.
9. Holiday travel – plan - be sure to travel from an airport at a reasonable time.
10. Being nervous – plan - get friends to pray for you.
11. Computers – plan - get friends to help you.

Your list may be totally different from mine but just putting things down helps amazingly. Try it!

11

Create Small Pleasures and Do Things Just For Fun

Jesus said he came to bring us abundant life. It's ours to be enjoyed. Just think of that parallel between a daddy and his little child. A daddy will go off to work in the morning delighted if his toddler hugs and smiles at him. A good daddy will take immense pleasure in seeing his little one happy, and only removes him from the scene when what appears to cause joy will actually endanger him.

Our heavenly Father wants to see us enjoying the life he's given us. He just loves us to bits. I heard the story of the businessman on the train opening up his laptop and there for his screen saver was a picture of his son. "Look at this," he says to a colleague also commuting to work. And he shows him, not one photo, not two but photos on end that he used as his screen saver until his colleague was quite bored. God has each one of us as his screen saver. He is not a 'kill–joy', he just loves to see us happy.

Therefore I see nothing wrong in a little planning to ensure ourselves special pleasures. If you absolutely adore cream cakes or custard slices or chocolate gateau, but know you shouldn't eat them all the time and can't stop, why not make a habit of allowing yourself one, say on a

Sunday, or Saturday night with the telly? Yes, I know this requires a bit of discipline, but you don't need to buy a pack of four!

This last June, I have enjoyed strawberries from my garden every single day. I often creep out in my pyjamas to pick them, and pile them onto my muesli! The strawberries used to be at the very top of the garden. It's a long garden, and takes a whole minute to walk up to the top. Not a great incentive to have instant strawberries for breakfast. So I moved the plot right next to my conservatory. So when I watch Wimbledon I can have strawberries for free! That's just one pleasure I have engineered, created for myself, and life is the lovelier for it.

Do you enjoy having fresh cut flowers around the house but your garden doesn't afford enough for you to pick at every season of the year? Why don't you give yourself a small 'flower allowance' each week? I had the idea to ask my daughter for a 'flower voucher' for my birthday, and then when I really wanted to buy flowers I could do so with the joy of spending my token! She gave me £15 and I got real bargains! There was the slightly less than fresh stocks for £3 a bunch and, oh what aroma filled my hall! They lasted five days. Next I chose lilies. Five days later these buds had not opened so I was just about to take them back to my man on the market but they blossomed and again perfumed my hallway. I really enjoy gerberas as well. However I shouldn't need a flower voucher. An average of £3 a week does not dig into my savings, as I'm really quite thrifty on things. So I say to myself, and to you, we must treat ourselves.

Get imaginative! Do you get transported by the beauty of birdsong but it isn't always the weather to sit out? You can buy CD's of birdsong... DVD's of wildlife.

Bring nature in and enjoy it audibly. Life need not be so 'spartan'.

If you long for a chocolate bar, make yourself wait for it. You'll enjoy it all the more. You have your 'to do' list. Well, after about the next six items listed, put 'have chocolate bar'.

Do you have the sudden urge to see the sea, and would not go to the trouble of driving there. Look up some day coach trips. It's an adventure. Also, if you are in easy train distance of London or a big city, treat yourself to a city day. It doesn't have to cost a lot. When I look for the stimulus of a London day, I take a packet of juice, some cheese, a roll and some fruit, enjoy walking round exciting new territory, go to a free museum, so that the only expense I have is a coffee or a tea! At our age we need not be slaves to the need to buy everything we want to put in our mouths!

Yes, and being very frugal, I think ten times before I replace anything I've got. However, when I saw that a king size duvet cover and pillowcases of a gorgeous design that would complement the colours in my room, only cost £15, there was no looking back.

So go for treats! Maybe you think that it is a childish concept, and that we have to be serious, responsible, wise, old people. Jesus' words ring in my brain, "Except you become like little children, you cannot enter the Kingdom."

Of course I may be writing to people who indulge themselves all the time and get a bit weary of it. Have I written a discipline chapter? Not as such but it is a constant thread through the narrative.

One guest on my weekly Christian radio show is a minister of the United Reform church. He is also a keen member of a local operatic society, and he was telling me on air that he believed that those of us who love God should not keep our lives serious all the time. We should have fun. Another leader of a local church has created a pottery and is often to be found there.

Jesus promised us abundant life and we shouldn't short-change ourselves.

I well remember a really fun-filled holiday. It was my first holiday after David had died. We were in Malta and it was a Christian group I had joined. There were talks at the end of the day; I had to keep my criticism under control, as I wanted much more Holy Spirit excitement about it all. No, I didn't want ranting and raving but a little more encouragement of the heart, rather than of the mind.

But I remember one outing. We went by coach, and in this place we were all having coffee together and just outside there were donkey rides. My childhood was spent near Dudley Zoo - in fact we had a season ticket there so could go every day; I had actually ridden on a camel and marvelled at sitting on a heated cushion. However, where we went for our seaside holidays it was wild Welsh countryside and beach, so that candyfloss, beach huts and donkeys were not part of our scene. That meant I had never ridden on a donkey.

This recently bereaved lady thought that riding a donkey would be fun. So I was heaved up, and hardly had I pressed the coins in the owner's hand when I was away... clutching hat, bag and change, and hoping I could stay on. That donkey certainly had a mind of its own. Perhaps he was hungry, because though he rode the correct course, he overtook my friend on another donkey. This was exhilarating. This was fun, and I even thought that I might take to riding a horse at some point.

Please don't suggest fairground rides, as I would surely be sick, but I've just remembered a more recent fling of mine. I was visiting my daughter, for Christmas, in Nottingham. On Christmas Eve afternoon we thought we'd pick up the buzz of the town centre, which was in walking distance of her house. It was actually a bit disappointing, as a lot of shops were closing at four, but in the central square was a traditional fairground ride of galloping horses. That was just enough of a thrill for me - I just loved the sensation and didn't begrudge the money, as I often do. It was lovely.

When I was watching the television the other day, there was a natural life programme that included the chough. The chough is a quite a rare bird, and I remember my father was thrilled to spot one on holiday in Wales many, many years ago. However, what fascinated me was that the chough flies in amazing patterns, not to catch food or to warn his enemies or to alert his chicks to where he is. He does it just for fun!

Opposite my house is a paddock of ponies. There are just three of them including Obie, a very short and obstinate grey miniature, and I often see them galloping around the field, tossing their manes. Why do they do it? Just for the sheer joy of it.

I like dancing. I did tap dancing as an adult though had to stop at Bronze level as I couldn't remember the sequences any more. I go to ballroom classes now though my poor memory is still the factor holding me back. However, get some exciting music on in the house and I'm kicking my legs up, showing off no end but just to nobody, just for fun.

What do you do, just for fun? Why not learn to giggle again! Laughter brings healing. If you are not well, get some DVD's out that will make you chuckle and roar with laughter. Laughter is known to give your whole mind and body a boost, effecting healing.

Catch New Things Each day and Pass Them On

Now you and I may have been alive for over fifty years or more, but the world is full of surprises. Have you been listening to a radio programme and said, "Well, I didn't realise that!"

Although I sing and enjoy musicals and some opera, when I happened to spend ten minutes looking at a world singing competition chat, they explained that two different techniques were needed when singing either an ordinary song or an operatic aria. In the opera you were a character and it was broad brush stuff. In a song, you had to convey all sorts of emotions and meanings just to bring this one song to life.

Here's another fascinating fact that I only learnt when I visited Hampton Court in the cold part of last autumn. In Tudor, and maybe medieval times, the pastry on pies, was only to hold together the little meal within – the venison or the rabbit or the vegetables, though I think meat was the dish of choice. You would receive your pie, hack your way into it, and eat the contents, almost using the crust as a covered casserole dish. But hey! There's no washing up involved as you just throw the pastry away. I'm amazed! To me the crust and its blend with the softer contents make the perfect texture and flavour to the dish.

Look out for new things to learn each day, and I don't mean that you have to master chess or memorise a Shakespeare sonnet. Just grab hold of a new fact that illuminates the world a little and delight in it. It may just stick in your mind. It may move you to write a poem.

I was travelling on the tube down to St. Pancras and though it wasn't rush hour there were a lot of us after that 9:30am dividing line into cheaper fares. As it was a fast train, I wasn't too worried about standing propped up for twenty minutes. We'd not long started when my eyes went down to the floor. An ant was running along. I say running but it wasn't getting that far very quickly, and I wondered where he was heading for. Oops! A man moved his leg. No, the worst had not happened, the ant was still on the move, but by the time we got to Radlett, the next stop, he had disappeared. Now that ant really got me thinking. Was he aware of the sudden doom that he narrowly missed? We humans were to him more than giants, almost like God, and that did set me off on the following poem!

I suddenly saw it.
It was moving down the carriage
A black speck!
The 9:33... yes...
It was packed to overflowing
We stood there
BUT THE
Audacity of it
We could crush him with a toe
In silence
As giants we towered
But now moving on to Radlett
He moved on.
A trainer then threatened
And I feared for his existence.
But why so?
I pour boiling water
On the ants nest in the garden
With no qualms.
Its 'cos of his bravery- Tchianamen square scenario.
I honour him.
Does God see us likewise? Are we too small to count?

In actual fact I enjoy people - watching - probably more so now that I'm in my later life. I don't always want to be head down in a book. When I was working in London, just off Baker Street, and travelled down from Stanmore, I used to get off one train and almost automatically get onto another, with my book still glued to my nose. I might even be writing a letter and have that on the go. Wow, that does date me. Who writes letters now? I enjoyed letter writing and found the train a good place to do it, as my first line could always be, 'I am writing this on the train going to... '

But people are always fascinating. What do their eyes say? Are they sad or worried or anxious or resentful?

Ask yourself a question at the end of the day. What was good about today? Don't dwell on mistakes and failures. What new and delightful thing did I learn?

Catch a new thing each day.

Don't neglect the small joys, literally. I've just been on a walk with Ros, a friend of mine. She has an eagle eye and knowledge of the natural world of flowers and butterflies that far surpasses mine. I think we must have seen five different species of butterflies, about thirty different wild flowers, on our forty minute walk. She'd spot tiny wild flowers.

"Black Horehound," she'd murmur.

"Pick that leaf and smell it!"

"Ugh!.. Terrible!.."

"Small things can be fascinating."

Live for others

Here's another slant on daily surprises. Maybe do a new thing for someone else each day and feel the joy of it.

We get back to God's rhythm for us which we have structured into days and weeks and years. We have the seventh day rest, the seventh year jubilee, the day and night.

Is it the Brownies who should do something helpful each day? Anyone remember 'Bob a Job' week? Well, it's actually in holy writ that we are here to do good deeds. "Let us consider how we may spur one another on toward love and good deeds." (Hebrews 10 v 24)

Our church has a ministry called Vineyard Active. Teams involved give time on a Saturday or evening to doing jobs for others in the community, which they can't do themselves. I had a young man spray paint my fifteen trellis fences, as I found the pressure required in operating it a bit too much.

But in later life we may not be able to do big manual things for others. Here's an idea, along with discovering new things each day: Why not ask God each day for some way in which we can please and surprise someone else?

I suppose that should mean taking a bit more time for your journey to town by car. Just think of the ripple effect of letting a car waiting at a side road, go in before you. The smile and gesture will be passed on. It could mean so many random acts of kindness.

I always try and chat to the people on the supermarket checkouts. If they're young they might be getting money for their university place. If they are older they mostly have families. It could be a pretty boring job.

You don't have to rack your brains to think of ideas. Just let the fragrance of Jesus be sensed about you as you pick up God's idea that pops into your brain. You don't need training in how to love others, it'll be there in your heart if you let Jesus pour his love through you, and he'll give the ideas.

It does not matter that this kindness encounter does not lead to showing them a booklet on how to become a Christian. You do your bit, and God will follow it up with other Christians interacting with them.

Living for others does not have to be a taking up of your cross or laying down your life. The joy you receive when you have been able to help someone far exceeds the inconvenience of it.

What gives you the greatest joy in life? On the Radio 4 programme, 'Any Questions', a questioner asked, "Who do you think is happier, a cleaner or a banker?" There was a range of answers offered.

Joy is different from happiness. What for you is the greatest joy? I think I could list a few options. I could consider people honouring me on my birthday, or going to an opera, or being treated to a meal, or getting an article in the paper, or performing well in a musical. These are all thrills for me. However, the day when I truly feel most on top of the world is actually when I've able to say a little about Jesus to someone, or to bless them, or to help them in his name. My daughter says this is because I've the 'evangelist' gift but I wouldn't take it that far. You might have great joys through other things.

This chapter started off with discovering new things each day. I'm ending it with the aim of bringing Jesus to someone each day, in however small a fashion.

12

Ask Help from Everyone

How about these scenarios?

- You've been told how to crop photos on the computer. You've even found the instructions, but it doesn't work this time.
- You think that your plastic water barrel in the garden has very little water in it, but how do you open it up? The last time you got your next door neighbour round to do it; he just turned something, and looked at you as if you were a fool.
- It's dim in that corner of your lounge as you just can't get the old light bulb out.

Do you identify with those situations at all? I must say that I can get discouraged as I live alone, because I am not a 'do-it-yourself' sort.

For five months I thought my long fluorescent bulb didn't work and wouldn't go to the hassle of replacing it, then found there were two switches under the cupboard. First I had to switch on one then the other one worked.

Don't be surprised that this happens to you. My house is full of things that aren't quite functioning correctly, because there hasn't been the person I could ask to do the job.

Now this does not trouble me unduly as I am not a perfectionist. Any house-proud person could easily discover areas that have not been cleaned thoroughly. When I painted the walls of my broadcasting studio an interesting green, my interior decorator interviewee encouraged me to paint paler stripes down the walls as a feature using masking tape. I thought that quite an adventurous idea and had great fun with it. One or two of the stripes aren't quite straight, but that doesn't bother me in the slightest.

So I admit I may be very different from you, who hop up and down in frustration if everything isn't working exactly as it should be. However, you must take it in your stride that this is one of the down sides of later life on your own.

But here's a really positive thought.

Think how wonderful you are to make ninety five percent of your household stuff work. Your mother wouldn't have been able to do half of the stuff you can do. Encourage yourself. Then switch to doing something you are expert at, something very few people can do. "Who else can create mono prints with oil paint," I tell myself. For you it may be baking a Victoria sponge, or taking cuttings off plants and so creating new ones. It might be the old art of tatting, or even the skill of playing bridge or chess.

Realise that no one person is expert at everything. When I was single, I really felt that other people expected a lot more of me than they would of a married woman. They would expect me, and other single women, to present an attractive appearance, have all the time in the world to be social, yet also to clean my house and even change the car tyre on the motorway! No man would expect that of his wife.

Think of a church. If it is small, the man at the top does tend to feel that he needs to be a 'jack of all trades', leading worship, pastorally caring for his flock, promoting evangelism, doing a good sermon and keeping his eye on the financial affairs of his church. But that's where the Body comes in, supplementing its particular gifts with his own. In similar fashion, to manage everything a mature single woman might need to manage, she needs help from others.

Sink your pride and ask for help. Thinking of a TV programme I watch, there are certain times when you need to 'phone a friend'. I am fortunate in having lots of people coming into my house because I have about thirty child 'piano' pupils and a few adults. They feel like my friends as they are weekly visitors. So why not delay the piano pupil's dad with a small request. In my experience they are always happy to help.

Another idea is to put away your pride and pop next door. We are always reluctant to ask, but people actually love to help. My very practical neighbours – the husband, a plasterer, the wife, very hard working with two teenage sons – are always ready to go out of their way for me.

Do you belong to a small group in your church fellowship? You must realise that most people are happier to give help than to receive it. If you feel bad about asking, what about giving a 'thank you' present of something in your gifting. I sometimes paint pictures of people's pets which they are very happy to receive. Another treasured thank you is a bowl of gooseberries or blackcurrants from the garden.

The old idea of barter is not a bad one. Let's share the things that come easily to us, things of which we have in abundance, maybe in return for skills we don't have.

Cultivate friends

Sometimes, senior women sadly tell me that their friends are dying off now, yes literally, ending their life. Some bemoan the lack of friends but do nothing about it.

I agree that finding new friends when you are in your 60's and beyond is not easy. There is an old saying that 'old friends are good friends'. When I was at Exeter University, I found myself sharing a room with a Welsh girl, from Newport, studying Geography and Geology. I seem to remember that when she got up early to go on a geology expedition, I wanted to sleep on, and when I wanted to get up early to go to a prayer meeting, she wanted to sleep. That first year there was so much to discover, so much to learn, both about ourselves and about our reaction to the community around us. I really valued having a friend alongside.

It must be about forty five years later that this friend found my name on an internet site and we linked up again and we had been living quite close together, Hertford and St. Albans. She had been in children's publishing and I had done various things but was leading pre-school music groups and teaching piano. It was actually very relaxing to meet each other again. We were the same people. We had history together.

However much time elapses between meetings up, a really good friend stays that way, so if you feel the need for a close companion, look up old friends. When I consider who my friends are they vary in age from being fifteen years younger to fifteen years older. Age really doesn't matter.

13

What is Your Special Ministry?

What can you do for God that no one else can do? What is there that only you can do? I would advise you to treasure it, enlarge it, grow it and make it fruitful.

I like drawing, and quite often, if I'm quick at it, I can get a fair likeness of people. It's a good way of keeping yourself from the boredom of airports and station platforms. Of course, I have more studies of the backs of people's heads and side views than full frontal, as I don't usually ask their permission. At one time, when I was in a church where the message did not grab me, I'd write notes of the sermon on one side of my pad, and draw the silent heads of the congregation on the other.

It's a habit that I started young. I seem to remember that I used to draw the faces of all the relations who came for Sunday tea, when I was seven or eight.

I have never thought that drawing portraits was a gift that God could use. However this changed when I started to work with STEP, a Christian ministry working in secondary schools, with interns and volunteers taking lessons, assemblies and form times.

STEP works in lots of schools in the area, and quite intensively in a few schools where the opportunities are more numerous than the number of volunteers we have to help. STEP volunteers go in and teach lessons on such things as sex, abortion, green issues, the cross, Jesus etc. etc. and this work is highly appreciated by schools.

As I could only afford to give my Tuesday mornings, I was assigned to do form times with year 7's in this very welcoming Church of England school.

The first assignment of the day was at 8:15am with the Breakfast Club. This I found particularly difficult. I, an adult unacquainted with the school, had to walk into a room seething with fifty or seventy young people, and make meaningful contact with them. This was hard as they were chattering excitedly to their peers, or on their mobiles and sometimes bleary-eyed from their early start. I am a fairly open person but I found contact quite embarrassingly forced until I hit on the idea of using a skill God has given me of being able to sketch people quickly and get a reasonable likeness. You can imagine it. I started to draw one person and soon drew a crowd. Although I don't find it easy to chat while I am concentrating really hard on my drawing, it honours the youngsters, and I write a little 'God-thought' on it before I give it to them

As we do the same 'form time' six times with the six parallel forms, we work out the best way to put things over. The interns are usually 50 years younger than me so the presentation is not just handed out from a teacher-like older person

I can still contribute to sharing the gospel, with the generations to come, as Psalm 71 advocates. I only started doing this about two years ago.

There must be inter-denominational schemes in most cities and towns, to bring the gospel into schools. Winkle them out, and if this can be your thing; forget how old you are and enjoy the alertness and honesty of talking about Jesus with children and young people. They won't

let you get away with traditional notions that you can't
back up with current examples

What's your gift?

There are all sorts of ways to work out your gifting
and personality. It's fun doing Myers Briggs questions,
and colour challenges.

- Are you an outward person, able to chat to the
  person next to you on the bus?
- Are you a listener, like someone I met today who
  knows her gift and rejoices in it?
- Are you a far-sighted thinker, who can assess
  situations objectively?
- Do you love cooking?
- Can you cope with very small children for an hour
  or two?

From even this small list can come so many ways of
serving God by serving others. If you haven't got a God-
given ministry, just keep on asking God and see what you
are comfortable doing. He made us exactly as he wanted
us, and if we let him, he is still working on transforming
us, so there must be a 'you' type service for him that you
can do.

If you are serious about wanting to know what God
wants you to do, grab uninterrupted time to get apart with
God, maybe early in the day when no one rings you or
lunch time in the park or late at night.

There's advice about managing your gifting in Peter's
first letter:

"Each one, as a good manager of God's different
gifts, must use for the good of others the special gift he
has received from God."

What is your special gift that God has given you? Have you worked it out yet? Look back on areas in which you have excelled and look to God for different gifts he may be giving you for the future.

You are never too old to take on something different, if that's God's path for you. He will probably heighten a gift that's been latent in you for some time but don't rule out the possibility of a change of direction in God's service.

Then, when you start to get excited about something you'd like to do for him, but it's not yet the right time, or it's not possible right now, hold that vision in your heart, let Jesus continually refresh it, and hang in there until its realised. Another lovely lady told me recently that her dream was to work in the secular world – in the City, as it happens - for money, two days a week, then to work two days a week for charity, and have one day off at home. That is now precisely what she is doing. God delights in the vision you have and he gives the vision in the first place.

You Can Still be an Evangelist

Yes we have the remit for this, even from the Old Testament. Take in this quote from Psalm 71:

Psalm 71:17-18
You have taught me ever since I was young
And I still tell of your wonderful acts.
Now that I am old and my hair is grey,
Do not abandon me, O God!
Be with me while I proclaim your power and might
To all generations to come!

'Proclaim your power and might' could mean teaching believers, or it could mean witnessing to the rest of the world. 'To all generations to come' implies younger people than us.

Here are some ideas.

1. **Get alongside younger people -** there are more opportunities than you realise.

In the days when this psalm was written, I'm sure old age was venerated much more than it is today. In the Middle East the old are honoured today much more than in Britain. What the elderly say to their children, and grandchildren, and extended family, counts.

However, as this is God's Word, I think we can apply it to ourselves. Don't think that teaching the children in the church must only be left to the young. Maybe there is the place for you to volunteer to go into schools as part of a Christian venture.

2. **Get talking in love, everywhere you go -** asking about the other person at the bus stop, or the cash till etc. You never know, God may open an opportunity.

I think generally that we are freer to be ourselves when we move on in life. We are no longer afraid to say 'no' to a request for babysitting, or an invitation out to dinner with people who are actually really boring company. Yes I know God might want us to make an inroad there, but you know what I mean.

We are no longer 'chary' at asking the meaning of a word or a concept. If I, at my age, haven't heard of this thing, then it must be very technical, very new, or I am walking in a totally different society from normal. I am not afraid of being different, for example, if I get really tired by 10:30pm, then I say so and move off back home.

This freedom to be oneself actually works well for the gospel, for spreading the good news. Most strangers who sit in silence around us are really appreciative of a few words. The bus pass is an excellent institution if you have the time. The first opportunity is when you are waiting for a bus. You have the perfect opening gambit. "Have you been here long? Has the 303 gone?" There's great camaraderie in shared minor misfortune.

Then when you are actually packed into the bus with the younger people attached to mobiles or ipods, you might find another senior person to whom you can comment on the weather. This remains a good old English starter. There are others. You could comment on the latest news, or enquire whether the bus stops at such and such a place. It's just amazing, when Jesus Christ is in you, and you really want his glory, you don't have to try, his fragrance just happens to spill out. You get out of the bus thinking, "Well, how did we get round to talking about church, or bereavement, or what's valuable in life?"

We may just make someone smile! Isn't that a gift we can hand out liberally? The other day, in a queue in the central post office, the kind that has lots of cashiers, and the Voice that says, "Cashier number six please"... a large, but fairly young, lady with unkempt hair came behind me and said, "Is it moving?" She meant the queue. I reassured her but she was hovering and rolling from one wide leg to the other, and almost trying to overtake me. When I was at the front I turned to reassure her. "We're nearly there." "Oh," she said, "good! I'm in a dreadful hurry." Then I said something that in my normal frame of mind I would never say as I get very impatient in queues, "Would you like to take my place?" And she flashed me such a surprised look, and then a 'thank you' afterwards. That must have been Jesus inside of me coming out of me despite me.

Then there was the time when my friend and I had a London day out and went on a guided walk, a favourite pastime of mine. The guide, who was probably an out-of-work actor, told such fascinating anecdotes that it just brought the locality to life. We were at Warwick Avenue and after we'd walked by the canal, we wanted somewhere to eat our sandwiches, not being extravagant enough to frequent cafes. We were walking along a very wide road with palatial white stucco houses as far as you could see. We'd been told that these were residences once occupied by royal mistresses and a famous composer lived next door. The road was so wide that there was plenty of room down the centre for parking and taxis, but sadly no little walls for us to perch on. At last we spotted a park bench. It was the only park bench for as far as you could see left and right and it was occupied. "Oh, there's just one man; there's room for us," I said, and we bustled off to sit down next to him, and he politely shuffled along.

As I took out my lump of cheese and my roll, I peered out of the corner of my eye to see what this man was reading. You'd never guess - it was a Bible! Mark's Gospel! I did a double take inside myself and then actually started a conversation with him something along the lines of, "Can't help noticing you're reading Mark's gospel."

I had assumed he was a Christian but when starting to ask him whether he was or not, something prompted me to say "or perhaps you are searching for the truth." And, do you know, he was in the latter category. Now we didn't know any churches in this part of London, so God brought to my mind that I should encourage him to look for an Alpha sign, and then try that church. He knew what I was talking about. Phew, think how God had directed us!

One lengthy road inhabited by the fabulously rich! One small, rather broken down, park bench! What a God-incidence!

And I think, as we weren't young girlies wanting to chat him up, it was in order; it was okay to be bold and initiate a conversation with him.

3. **Check who you see regularly -** if you only see Christians regularly, get out and do a class or hobby with other people e.g. ballroom dancing, walking, table tennis etc.

I mentioned my ballroom dancing class every Thursday evening. The men move round every few minutes. So during an evening I probably dance with most of the men there, and I start to talk. Now you must know that if you're a Christian, what you do and your attitude to any subject that comes up is coloured by the light of Christ within you. This is not the trigger to opening up your handbag to find a booklet on how to become a Christian, but if you lead a life of continual prayer, (that is if you are in constant contact with your Saviour with the Spirit breathing his life through you) then you never know what might happen.

Of course you can be part of a team to hold open air services or healing on the streets, or even go door knocking (why is that out of favour?) but if you see your un-churched friends often, then almost in spite of yourself, somehow a glimpse of Jesus will come out of you.

What interests you in life? Do you watch every news bulletin and have your own opinions on the Middle East or Europe? Find others who like debating politics, or even join a political party.

Do you enjoy gardening but only have a small plot? See if any allotments are available. Do you enjoy painting at home? Maybe the light of Jesus in you would be doubled if you took part in a painting class and interacted with others.

There are groups supporting Alzheimer's sufferers; there are charity shops that might need your help.

Even if you conclude that your ministry is intercessory prayer which can be done at home, you can go where people are and pray for them in situ.

I believe as Christians today we are too complacent. You may live in a village but a lot of us are in reach of towns where several churches flourish. How much influence is the body of Christ having on your locality? At one time I was working for the African Inland Mission, setting up their new office and editing their magazine. I remember vividly being told that in Algiers, there were seven known Christians. No, not seven churches, just seven individuals! Compare that with us in Britain. We must take care that we don't come under the condemnation of being 'luke warm'.

I have long had an imaginative plan that will probably never come to fruition. I plan that at a certain agreed time on a certain date, all those who were true believers in Jesus should step outside their houses onto the pavement. I think we'd get surprises galore! I reckon that there'd be roads where crowds of people would look around in amazement at each other, not knowing they lived there, as their church paths didn't cross!

So again I ask: What is your ministry?

It may not be the same one as you had ten years ago or thirty years ago. Remember too, that the numbers of over 60's will be increasing in the next years, and with all the modern medical discoveries, we'll all be living even longer. This means that our peers need to be told about Christ, one way or another, or we are failing them.

14

Save Money and Give it Away

Now amazingly, my husband and I never fell out about the important things, like where to go on holiday, which house to buy or money.

David was generous. I love the fact that he once said, "Let's give a thousand pounds to the really poor in our church, without them knowing." It was such fun to effect. Actually you need to be prepared not to be thanked at all, but I did rejoice in one reaction, because this lady shared with me how God had blessed her, and she never knew it was me.

Practise being thrifty

I have always been thrifty. I suppose being a child in the 1940's in a middle class home taught me that. We had really comfy rag rugs on the floor. Rag rugs were made out of weaving strips of cloth through a canvas webbing base, and the strips of cloth came from our outworn clothes if the garments didn't go down the other route, into dusters. Yes, as an adult it came as a surprise to me that people would bother to buy yellow dusters.

I went to university in an age when the state paid for your accommodation and fees, but sometimes your parents' income demanded a small contribution, as in my case. However, when I did a fourth year out, a post grad in librarianship at Loughborough, I didn't pass on the forms for them to supplement my bursary. I just did without.

Later I changed jobs from being a local history librarian with a mortgage on a lovely little house, and a car, to editing the North Africa Mission magazine and helping set up the Loughborough office. This halved my income, so I gave up the car for a bike but still managed to pay the mortgage!

So I've had lots of practice on joyfully living on less!

Practical tips on saving money

There are so many ways of saving money. You can't get out of the council tax, or your income tax, or keeping your hair looking well groomed. However being assiduous on cleaning your teeth is a saver. I discovered that my dentist was asking me to make appointments with a hygienist, which cost, what £45 or £50 a time. I thought this usual, until a year later there was no more talk of hygienists, so much less cost. The reason was that I was spending much more time and expertise on my teeth, with electric toothbrush, floss, mouth wash etc. A minute extra each time saved me a considerable amount. You can probably think of other examples.

The other day I decided to walk round a small local lake and park. You used to be able to park in their car park out of season freely, but now there's a compulsory charge of about £2 per visit, however long you stay. But I remember with husband, daughter and dog that we found a very wide road where we could park easily, only 4 minutes walk away. So that's what I do now.

In fact my visits to my local town are governed by the parking restrictions. Outside a certain school there is free parking between 9:30am and 3:00pm. so there's a few of us, a bit like a club, who get there from 9:20am onwards to obtain our places, keeping a sharp look out for the yellow and blue uniform of the parking attendant.

Free food and travel

Now here's another way of saving money which is also very ecologically sound and good for your health.

Just now it happens to be late August and 'fruit and veg' are maturing in our gardens. However, just go out to any local hedgerows - you don't have to be in the country – and you'll find blackberries. Pick them, rich in nutrients, free. Add them to your breakfast cereal, as I did strawberries from the garden in June, as I mentioned previously. If you see 'freeze dried fruit' as highlighted on a cereal packet, think of the tortuous process the poor strawberry has gone through. Fresh is best.

I was clearing up one part of the garden the other day and found that my neighbours were out in their garden as well. My pear tree was groaning with fruit and as I discovered they like their pears crisp, a bucket of pears went over the fence in exchange for some runner beans. Now that is the good life on a scale I can manage. I still have a car as I am in a semi-rural part of the country. However, I must make myself use my free bus pass more often. I have a friend who I could call a 'bus master' of the area, who enjoys shopping and museums in several towns near here, all thanks to the bus pass.

Plan to give

If you're going to enjoy later life, you need to be in control of your finances as I have covered in the chapter 'Manage Well'.

If you honour God and put him first, he will always give you enough to give away and his generosity in this way will not stop when you are that bit older, and probably on a small pension.

Being thrifty where necessary leaves me free to respond to God's call when he asks me to donate money here or there. That is a delight. Sometimes I feel a God nudge that I have a thousand pounds in that building society and I need to give it to such and such a cause. Now you have to know me to know that I am probably not generous by nature. I am strict on my own spending and I never look forward to a situation, say in a pub, where I have to stand the round of drinks.

But when God says do it, somehow there's an inexplicable joy about it and I never lose out.

I have to stop myself grumbling about the council tax, which is usually the largest outgoing on my monthly bank account. I feel strongly that it is unfair that local tax is levied on the basis of houses. There could be four wage earners in a reasonably small house, with one lot of council tax to pay or, like myself, one person in a family house, enjoying it to the full, but not even earning. Yes I have a 'bee in my bonnet' about that, that local tax should be income-related, but as a Christian I must accept the status quo.

If you've never done it, sit down with your accounts and work out how much money comes in, how much has to go out, and how much you can give to God in different ways and to other people. Tithing is a much used bench mark, and some churches think that the tithe ought to go to them, and that the 'offerings' mentioned in the Bible are what you ought to give to other charities etc. I think you should just ask God and do what feels right. His Spirit is in you. Decide on how you want to give, and do it.

I personally do not have a credit card. I do not want to be in debt. When we had a store card, I used to be really upset that a month later I discovered that we had not yet paid for that carpet or that washing machine.

Random acts of kindness

I have great fun in giving. We are told to be 'hilarious' givers, and I think if we wince as we give generously, that is not being generous.

The phrase 'random acts of kindness' is quite in vogue just now. I always like to think of the people on the check-outs as human beings, and so like to chat to them. One lady really worried me by doing her work so fast that I commented, and she said that management had told them they had to speed up. So that meant less time to chat to customers. Well, I'm afraid I take the initiative and chat to them. This is especially helpful in a small or moderately sized super market where you do see the same people again.

Sometimes the name on their badge is an opportunity to chat: "Oh, Zamberia! What an interesting name, does it mean something?" One lady, when I asked her how she was, seemed quite sad and confessed that it was the anniversary of her husband's death so not a good day. I sympathised, but it was only when I'd got home that I realised what I should have done. So the next time I went there, I bought a bunch of sweet smelling stocks, only £3 worth, I recall, and happily managed to get to this lady's check out. So when all was paid, I said, "Oh yes and these are for you!"

In the Gospels we even read that Jesus said use money to make friends for yourselves! How do we unpack that? Does he mean bribing? I hardly think so, but here's another idea that some Christians have done and I have tried. Decide to treat someone in your hairdressers to a free hair do. Just say at the cash desk when you pay, "Oh and I'll pay for her as well." It certainly gets a surprised reaction. It's so contrary to the ways of the world that hopefully someone will notice and relate it to Jesus. You could also do this in a restaurant.

Have you ever seen a 'Big Issue' seller in your town? Ours at the moment, George, is a gentle Christian guy from Romania and he's really struggling. He was very concerned that he couldn't get money for his five year old's school clothes. On investigation, this was only £12.99! Sometimes he only sells six magazines a day!

I remember the lead pastor in our church saying how in a supermarket queue the woman in front of him held them all up till they were 'tut tutting' like anything, as she had only got a card to pay for her goods, and not cash, and this was a cash-only supermarket. The queue got longer, the shoppers more impatient, and in the end he said, "Look here, I'll pay for her," and that was a true random act of kindness. Apparently the cashier started to cry and everyone applauded.

God prompts me

I must say that I am happier paying the fiver, the tenner or the thousand if God actually digs at me to do so, rather than giving a generous tip at restaurants. I have yet to learn that. It's the thrifty part of me rising to the top when it shouldn't. Although, come to think of it, I can't remember when I last ate at a restaurant. We need to cultivate a listening ear to hear his prompts.

The other day I bought a couple of bunches of daffodils to brighten up my home. On the way back, however, I was visiting the head of a nursery. Just as I was parking my car, that voice in my head that I am growing to recognise, said, "Give her the flowers." I am also learning to obey promptly. It's much easier than wrestling with the, "Did he, didn't he?" discussion inside my head. It also means that next time God speaks I discern it more clearly.

So there's the need to give. There's the need to save. Then there's the need to spend. It doesn't glorify God if you keep it all saved up. Remember the story of the man who stored up all his stuff into barns for the years to come? Don't get me wrong, I have savings for my old age, and these are controlled and regulated, but I still have enough to spend on myself and others

We can all be secret givers, out of the wealth and time that God has given us, whether it be a little or a large amount.

15

Save Time and Give it Away

Now you might think that saving time is the last thing that a senior person would want to think about. You might have such quantities of time, that you are longing for more company and more things to fill up your days. However, if you are active and seeking to live in God's purposes, you must want the time you spend on various tasks to be valuable.

I want to save time, money and energy to spend what I have in the most satisfying profitable way. I want to cut corners for a lovelier life.

There are duties and tasks that have to be done. Why do you need to fill up your days with them? You are worth more than that. You have 'giftings' that God can use, that are invaluable to him. Even if you are in your late 80's and 90's enjoying being still and spending time in quiet contemplation, you can fill your time with prayer, interceding for what God puts in your mind. You can also draw other people into your ambience, so that they catch the Holy Spirit in you, glean your God-sense, and have an available ear to receive all the troubles concerns and joys that other lonely people wish to pour out.

So I am suggesting that the necessary things are done, and indeed done to the glory of God.

"Whatever you do, whether you eat or drink… do all to the glory of God," (I Corinthians 10 v31) but they do not always have to be done in excess. I agree that your seedlings on the shelf need to be watered daily, and that you need to see that you are well groomed.

I suggest, however, and I know, that many house-proud people will exclaim in horror at what I am going to say, that you don't always clean the house with extreme thoroughness. I always look for short cuts in the non-creative tasks needed in my house.

Short cut on laundry

For example, I am a widow, and therefore luxuriate in the same king size bed that I shared with my late husband. I really enjoy leaving my Bible and reading matter on the other half of the bed! But when it comes to washing, that duvet cover is massive. It pretty well fills up the whole of one wash, maybe with a small towel tucked in! Do I need to wash it every week? Well, yes, the part near my face, probably, especially if like me you enjoy breakfast in bed. But one morning I had a 'eureka' moment thinking about this duvet cover. Nothing was soiling the other side of it, and my feet didn't really come down to the bottom, therefore I could rotate my duvet round each week, and only wash it after four weeks! Are you shocked? Well, I'm enjoying less work and saving a bit on electricity!

Short cut on washing dishes

Then there's the washing up. I have a dishwasher but the last time I used it, it wasn't as effective as it used to be. I live alone and although lots of people come into my house, for broadcasting, for piano lessons and for a cuppa now and then, I don't entertain for meals and always eat on my own.

When I used the dishwasher, I used up nearly all my crockery and cutlery about every 5 days. There it was stacked up in the dishwasher, the food dried on the plates, generally smelly and disgusting.

So now, unless I have an influx of people, I just put my dirty stuff in a bowl of water, and wash up... wait for it... not after every meal, but maybe once every day or every two days! That saves all the power you use for a dish washer, although my glasses might not be quite so sparkling. It's just one of those choices I have made in later life. I also find it's a useful chore to do when you are tired, maybe just before you go to bed.

Yes, and here's another tip about washing up. If you have saucepans to clean, just think about them – they are only dirty on the inside – so why wash all the outside as well and get all the dirty washing up water all around it. Just wash what is dirty! Interesting thought? Try it. That's a tip I got from a television programme.

Short cut on house cleaning

I do my house cleaning at the weekend, just once a week, and I'm sure you do what I do sometimes. I take intense care of my gas cooker hob and clean it all, or really get behind the appliances in the utility, or take lots of loving time sorting out my dressing table, but then I might get through the rest of the house very quickly. Oh the joys of a good sweeper!

Chat at same time as housework

I am just realising how to make certain parts of housework more interesting. Yes, there is the radio or the television if you're in the right room, but there's another way.

This morning, in the holidays with no piano pupils, and my holiday preparations well ahead, and no recording to do for my radio programmes I had the whole morning free. There was painting I wanted to do, but there was also a lot of housework as I like to leave the place clean before I go away. It makes for a much pleasanter return home.

By 11 o clock, I was missing people, as I sometimes do, and I'm not able to programme them in, morning afternoon and evening in holidays. So I thought I'd ring up some friends, and by doing so, get more house work done. Read on to discover how I do this.

First I rang up one friend but she was out. Then I rang up James in Chelmsford, who I only see about twice a year, and he was in and very happy to chat, as are most older people who live on their own. Now I have discovered that there is such a lot of kitchen cleaning you can do with one hand - the gas hob, for instance, the smears on the kitchen cupboards, the grime round the taps on the sink and you can think of plenty more places. So while I am being entertained by my friend and telling all my news, I am also getting the no-brainer cleaning done painlessly. That's the beauty of it! If that same friend was with me, of course I wouldn't be doing anything else but listening to him, but when they're on the phone I can get such a lot done.

Giving time

So I can cut non-essential corners and save time and then I have a little more time to give away.

It's another relevant form of giving. You may not have the funds or the inclination to be able to donate to every cause that puts its leaflets through the letterbox or pleads with you in the street but you may be able to give time.

Do I have enough spare time to help people out? Can I offer to do their shopping? Have I enough loose areas to serve other people? My own life is very full in term time with teaching piano and broadcasting and painting and maybe it should have a little more slack in it to be available for God to use me. If I am to enjoy later life to the full, I should not just be having a good time myself. I shall gain so much more satisfaction if I am able to give to other people. Maybe I should be willing to linger with a neighbour who needs to pour out their troubles at length, or accept that my friend on the phone needs to talk on and on.

Helping out with grandchildren

Should I be giving time to help my married children, perhaps giving them child care? In this century the very term 'childcare' smacks of official proscription, handed out by the state and having to be paid for. At one time, it was taken for granted that family members looked after other family members, whether it was a confused granny or tear-away two year old.

Now that more mothers are in paid occupation, and need to go back to work due to financial pressure, grandparents are more important in the help they can give.

I know one grandfather who travels to his daughter's house to look after three small boys really early in the morning and then takes them to school. This is because their dad is a postman on early duty, and their mum also has to travel some distance to her job. This is sacrificial! For every individual there is a choice to be made and a balance to be kept. In later life we mustn't have the attitude that 'now time is my own, and haven't I earned it through working all those years!' We mustn't be blind to a service that God may encourage us into.

16

Coping with Age-Related Minuses

The usual image of the older man or woman is that they have 'passed their sell-by date'. They are to be pitied, as their youthful strength gives way to illnesses of mind and body. The wisdom and glory of their successful business life, sporting fame, or creativity is undermined by the current presentation of the older figure.

I shall be fighting this with all my skill but I am aware that there are minuses of being in your 70's 80's or 90's. Here are a few that we need to recognise and cope with excellently.

1. Forgetting Names

I've mentioned this memory slip that peppers our social life. Why not read your address book or contact list regularly? Having the names in front of you reminds you that these friends exist and it really does help your memory when you need to recall someone.

2. Waking up in the night regularly

Probably by the age of 70 we need less sleep over night than we did. Also, a lot of us in this age group don't seem able to sleep through our six, seven or eight hours a night. I have found that for the last seven or eight years I have woken up at a regular time, usually at 3:30 am. It would be lovely, wouldn't it, to have a guarantee of sleeping through 'till morning but a 'night stop' is one of those age-related minuses, which we can turn it into a plus.

What do you do when you wake up? Do you glance at the clock, and think, "Oh, no!"? Try to react positively. You have options. One option is to trot to the toilet, have a drink of water and tuck yourself in again. Another, which usually gives me a definite hour of sleep is to wander down to my rebounder and gently bounce on it for a couple of minutes until my body is throbbing and then, before I know it, I'm awake again in the morning, hardly remembering that I went downstairs.

If my mind is particularly active, and all these ploys don't work, I go and have a nibble of something and a glass of milk, so that the blood which keeps your mind active is directed to your stomach. Well, that's what I've been told. Then I switch on the bedside radio.

Last night, however, I thought up something else. Awake at 4:30am, I felt full of praise to Jesus, so decided this must be top of my middle-of-the-night 'to do' list. I found myself, unusually, thinking of it as a gift to God, not as something to benefit me, and get me back to sleep, but something for him. Then it flashed through my mind that monks in monasteries used to, and maybe still do, wake up through the night at set times to go and say their liturgical offices. They are offering praise in the night time hours. For the first time ever, this made sense to me. In the night I could be productive spiritually.

The modern equivalent, of course, is the 24/7 prayer times that are organised in certain areas and for certain reasons. There is nothing new under the sun.

Because we are of a mature age, we can give even more back to God and turn this particular minus into a plus.

3. Coping with waiting

I am very fortunate in my good health. I do realise, however, that although the real me is internal, the body that encases it isn't. It won't go on forever. However much we try to stay young, there will be parts of our body that wear out a little, knees and hips to think of two.

This inevitably means appointments with medical people. I dislike appointments. Part of me feels that God should be healing me without all the incessant checking the 'powers that be' seem to want to do. I usually make the most of my time, and to sit around for thirty minutes or an hour when I could be doing much more interesting and beneficial, really frustrates me.

Waiting around is one of the down sides for me of growing older. I do need much more patience. Joyce Meyer wrote that impatience is the result of pride! We want to be seen straight away. It's our right! The opposite of pride is humility. One very brave friend, who had a kidney transplant, having spent much of her teenage years on dialysis, mentioned a phrase that I treasure. She said, "God is in the waiting!" Do I believe that? God is in the waiting.

Do I believe that I can use that 'in-between-time' fruitfully? There are books, and writing, of course, but take another look at the waiting room scene. Sitting around are a disperate collection of individuals probably all wishing they were somewhere else. Think of your appointment from God's point of view. He might be thinking, "Ah, Elspeth's got a mouth ulcer, that's unusual for her, but she's just the person I want to get Mrs Smith talking. Yes and old deaf Barty might like cheering up as well."

Although we don't really believe it, other people like being talked to and drawn out of themselves much more than we think. It's quite easy in a doctor's waiting room, and there's usually a common minor grievance, like the doctor being late and not on the premises yet, but then with a smile and God's ideas you can inquire about these people, ailing in body but so precious in God's sight, and you never know, you might get a God-word in!

The same goes for travel by public transport. Britain's upper lip is not as stiff as you think. I remember a train journey back from Nottingham to London, where the problem of our carriage being unheated brought us all into conversation, and I had a fascinating time with a published author sitting over the gangway.

'God is in the waiting'.

4. **Physical problems**

When you consider the usual image of an older person, they may be bent over, have difficulty walking, and have teeth and eye problems. We are indeed fortunate if our health holds out into our nineties. I have noticed in others that joints wear out – knees and hips – and also that teeth and eyes tend to degenerate.

We have to expect that our bodies could be wearing out. There is the old benchmark of 'three score years and ten!' and I think eyes and teeth are particular problems. I have an elderly neighbour who was fitted for dentures in her top jaw, but although she tried hard, could not get used to them, and does without. I myself, about eleven years ago, faced the fact that even the roots were rotten in four consecutive teeth. As I then led pre-school music, singing my way through the day, my husband and I together decided that it was worth spending money on implants. The year's process was not exactly pleasant but for ten years I have had really secure teeth in that area.

I think I would say in all these physical difficulties we shall probably face - be as kind to yourself as you can. Again, if we know God intimately, then we can discover all the options, take advice, but go forward in peace, coping with what discomfort any procedures or lack of them might produce.

Healing

There is always the possibility of healing. This is an area that we who have lived many years ought to be thoroughly investigating. This demands a book on its own. Suffice to say that I have in the last few months seen, yes actually seen, God relieve people of pain, and change their bodies with the laying on of hands of believing Christians, not just those who are ordained or trained for this service.

Maybe we accept our illnesses too readily as part of growing old. I haven't often heard of miracles of healing of the eyes, but one summer I was on a holiday in St. Ives, focussing on practising and preparing a Roger Jones' musical.

We were sitting and singing from our scores. Most of us wore glasses, as over the age of about 50, there is the need for magnification of small print. I personally have contact lenses, and rejoice in the sort called mono-lenses, which have a different prescription for each eye, one for short sight and the other for long sight. You wear them at the same time, and your eyes adapt to good sight both near and far. They are amazing.

I was sitting next to a lovely older lady who was probably in her eighties. She too was singing from her musical score, but she was not wearing spectacles. So in passing the time of day, I asked her if she wore contact lenses. Her whispered reply in between chorus singing was that she'd been healed. I was intrigued. Some time ago she had had a particular eye problem and God had healed her eyes. However, he hadn't just healed them to what was normal for a senior lady – good eyesight for her age - but obviously needing magnification for the small print. No! God had healed her sight so that she saw perfectly, even in old age.

Encouragement of seeing healings

That is a real encouragement to prayer. My late husband was healed of a major stroke pronounced by the hospital. I had seen him fitting on our lounge floor with one side of him convulsing. I cried out to Jesus, and to shorten the story, the next day every part of him was working, and they sent him home, now changing their diagnosis. He told me that when it looked bad from our point of view, he had seen an amazing bright light behind him, so that he daren't look round. Also, for several days at home after that, he woke up beaming with God's glow about him.

I must just finish the story. After he finally died of heart failure many years later, I went to get the death certificate from the Registrar - a daunting process. I glanced at it, and there was a list of illnesses they had deduced from the post mortem. One item said, 'Old cerebral enfarction'. I asked what that meant, and the registrar said, 'Old stroke.' I think I must be the only person receiving a death certificate who almost jumped for joy at the confirmation of my husband's healing.

That wasn't the only healing he received, but I want to emphasise that I am seeing healings now, like yesterday and last week. Sometimes people are not healed. I keep praying for the floaters in my eyes to drop down or disappear. To date they have not, but they are only minor irritations. Let's think big. We believe in God, a Creator, in Jesus a Saviour, in the Holy Spirit, empowering people today. Don't let the tradition of unbelief keep us from allowing his Spirit to do what he will in our bodies, sometimes bringing complete wholeness.

17

What to Expect in Your 80's and 90's

Now I regard myself as living a vibrant, creative life and I'm in nearly 70. I can't actually note any difference from ten years ago, except that I'm even more alive than I was. I suppose that forgetting names is one indication that my brain is losing a few bits.

Bodily, I have learnt the limits of my different limbs. I know by bitter experience that leaning forward high up to trim hedges can only be done for say, fifteen or twenty minutes at a time or my joints ache with the extra stress/usage. Also I remember that it was about seven years ago when I was told by my doctor that I had a frozen shoulder, and that was through scraping old paint off walls and not knowing when to stop, as the pain came a few days later. So probably in bodily terms, I am as fit as I was ten years ago, so nothing's changed there.

What about stamina, and needing a nap? Well, I now wake even earlier, and don't seem to need such long nights, so occasionally a ten minute nap after lunch revives me. However, this was just the same ten years ago.

I suppose in your 80s you ought to be considering the end of your life. Now, whereas some people in their

50's have already planned their funeral music, I haven't even contemplated where and when I will end my days. I'm too busy enjoying the current life.

Diana Athill in her book, 'Somewhere Towards the End', has very wise things to say regarding the very last years, but of course, as she didn't believe in an after-life she cannot look forward to anything.

Need for younger people around us

Diana, whilst honestly facing up to the more miserable aspects of old age, highlights an important need: that of having young life around us. Single people who have not been married are those who need to work hardest in this respect. They will not naturally have grandchildren to borrow and spoil. All of us should live in a mixed society as each age has something to give to the others. Do other less 'civilised' countries get it right in having the senior members of their family at the heart of their extended family? Would it work in Britain?

Some places, Nottingham for example, have purpose built villages for the over 60's. The residents are all senior citizens but there is a great gap from someone aged 60 to someone aged 95. The mix appears to work well. Should we isolate ourselves from young people and their small children, and teenagers? I'm not sure. The inhabitants of these villages for seniors seem to love it.

I teach piano to young children and really enjoy relating to them and their parents. In fact, when the school holidays come around, I find myself pacing the room at 4:00pm wondering what is wrong with my life. I've got so used to having young company for two hours.

Diana Athill sees the Importance of younger people 'flitting in and out of our awareness' when we are older, as a reminder of the whole cycle of life from birth to death.

I recognise that things have changed and will change further as my years increase. I do enjoy a freedom however. I have a freedom to say what I think, and not to be ashamed because I don't know anything. I don't have to show I am aware of modern life in the same way as younger people. I don't have to pretend to be accepted. I can be myself.

The emptiness on nothing to look forward to

I was passed the following poem which was found among the possessions of an old Irish lady who had died in a geriatric hospital, and reprinted from a newsletter of the Canadian mental Health Association.

CRABBIT OLD WOMAN

What do you see nurses, what do you see?
What are you thinking when you look at me?
Uncertain of habit, with far away eyes,
Who dribbles her food and makes not reply.
When you say in a loud voice, "I do wish you'd try."
Who seems not to notice the things that you do,
And forever is losing a stocking or shoe,
Who, unresisting or not, lets you do as you will.
With bathing and feeding, the long day to fill.
Is that what you're thinking, is that what you see?
Then open your eyes, you're not looking at me,
I'll tell you who I am as I sit here so still,
As I move at your bidding, as I eat at your will.
I'm a small child of ten with a father and mother,
Brothers and sisters who love one another.
A young girl at sixteen with wings on her feet,
Dreaming that soon now a lover she'll meet.
A bride soon at twenty – my heart gives a leap –

Remembering the vows that I promised to keep.
At twenty-five now I have young of my own,
Who need me to build a secure happy home.
A woman of thirty my young now grow fast,
Bound to each other with ties that should last.
At forty my young will soon be gone
But my man stays beside me to see I don't mourn.
At fifty once more babies lay round my knee.
Again we know children, my loved one and me.
Dark days are upon me, my husband is dead.
I look at the future, I shudder with dread,
For my young are all busy rearing young of their own,
And I think of the years and the love I have known.
I'm an old woman now and nature is cruel,
'Tis her jest to make old age look like a fool.
The body it crumbles, grace and vigour depart.
And now there's a stone where I once had a heart.
But inside this old carcase a young girl still dwells,
And now and again my battered heart swells.
I remember the joy, I remember the pain,
And I'm loving and living life over again.
I think of the years all too few — gone so fast,
And accept the stark fact that nothing can last.
So open your eyes, nurses, open and see,
Not a crabbit old woman, look closer — see me.
Need to be in own home.

What everyone wants is to live until the end in their own home, with the companionship of someone they love and trust.

Diana Athill again:

'I think that for people to look after their children when they are young, and to be looked after by them when they

are old, is the natural order of events — although stupid or perverse parents can dislocate it."

The sad thing is that for many of us, an unfortunate fall will take us to hospital, and often complications occur. At 93, my mother needed an operation on a stomach ulcer. She was offered the choice of having the operation or not having it. She chose to have it, and I personally think it was because she thought she wouldn't survive and so it would be a quick ending to life. However, my lovely soft-hearted mother must have had a tough physique, as she survived the operation, but not the various complications that came afterwards.

We can't all die at home. I trust that those of us who know Jesus can all die well.

The end

Diana thinks life is not pointless, that would be absurd, but she says:

"What dies is not a life's value, but the worn-out (or damaged) container of the self, with the self awareness of itself. The difference between being and non-being is so abrupt and so vast that it remains shocking."

I certainly found that, straight after my husband had died. We were away at a Shropshire conference centre, just beginning a week of 'castles, gardens and tea shops'. On the first day he was extremely slow on and off the coach, as we toured old churches discovering pagan gargoyles and other symbols of Christianity that wouldn't let go of pagan tradition. However, there were comfortable glimpses across the room as only two loved ones know, and I remember fetching him coffee while we watched slides of Stokesay Castle which we were to explore the next day.

David had recently been very restless in bed, and that night I said, "Oh David, we need to pray for a good night's sleep." I prayed a simple prayer. He retorted with a loud, "Amen." That was the last word I heard from him. I had a really good night's sleep, the best for a long time. I thought he had too, lying peacefully with his one arm over his head. When he didn't react to my rattle of the tea cups I went over to him and it was soon obvious he wasn't in his body.

Yes, I agree with Diana. There was an immense divide. I could no longer share anything with him. Last words had already been said. His last pudding of crumble with extra custard had been eaten. In no way at all could I have any more communication with my husband on earth. However, Diana's phrase a 'non-being' does not apply. His body was lifeless, but his life had moved elsewhere.

The period before the end

I understand that in our 80's we are not so active, but enjoy being more contemplative. We sit and take stock, or sit and doze. We sit and enjoy the memories of the past, or the beauties of people and nature in front of you.

I have already made firm decisions in my head regarding certain hospital treatments. I do not want people to strive officiously to keep alive. I have noted that in many cases the treatment for cancer causes more damage than the cancer itself. Why not enjoy the life you have, even if you are slipping towards the end, rather than cope with the block killing of parts of your body that is chemo and radio therapy? John Diamond, the journalist, wrote a book regarding his condition. They needed to take out his tongue!! As I write this I know that currently there is a lot of experimentation regarding injections to heal cancer, that are fast and effective without the side effects of chemo or radio therapy, but that's not a common option just yet.

But really old age is for the Christian the path up to heaven. In my experience, really old people either get sweeter or really sour! It's the fragrance of Christ in one who believes that makes all the difference. I think I ought to extract all the words in the Bible about heaven and the good things afterwards, and make them my daily meditation.

I found that since the time David's body died and his real self went to heaven, my thoughts and my imagination have worked over-time. Some people think of heaven as a continual praise party. I wonder about the non-musical believers there. I would enjoy a glorious praise session with thousands exalting Jesus, but I would not enjoy it endlessly, non-stop all day. I think the human being is created for variety and I remember CS Lewis' image of a door going into a place that was larger inside than outside. Shades of Dr. Who. I could imagine walking along through the countryside with three friends and the conversation being as satisfying as a meal of bread and honey and tasty casseroled meat! We would not upset each other, we would all be honoured and we would bounce humour off each other. Oh yes, in the broader perspective, I understand that every skill we have in the natural on earth is enlarged and enhanced and always culminates in success.

We must get into our heads that this life is only the prologue to the play, the real thing. It's just the overture to the opera, for which we were destined from before our birth. I read the other day in Psalms, 'God existed before time'. Yes, and that's the Psalm that says that those who love God will be like trees that stay green and produce fruit in old age. Oh to be fruitful in my 80's and 90's. The ladies in my family seem to live long lives - dying at 93, 95 and 97.

Aged parents or aunts

Because in Britain, at least, we are all fairly prosperous compared with a hundred years ago, and we do have some benefits and help from an NHS care system; even if some people slip the net, there are considerably more really old people living today.

This means that a young 70 year old, like myself, might be caring for a parent or aunt who is 90 or 95. We are enjoying later life, but still have the burden of care for people we love who are more senior than ourselves. I can imagine people, in their 70's themselves, getting worn out by caring for those in their 90's.

•

Once more, if God is in the equation, there should be a balance in caring and being cared for. I don't have any other answers other than that. We who are just in later life can prepare for older age in several ways:

- We can keep our body fit and another chapter deals with that side of things.
- We can keep full of the Holy Spirit and so spiritually fit.
- We can discover God's purposes through us and join him in their execution.
- We can feed the mind and imagination with expectations of heaven. These are indeed 'great expectations' building up to a crescendo of delight in the near future.

18

Turning Aloneness into God Time

Now ever since I've lived away from my childhood home, I've always found Bank Holidays difficult. I only married when I was 38, so I had plenty of adult Bank Holidays to cope with. Families and other people seemed to do special things on Bank Holidays, whether it rained or not. I found that nothing seemed to come my way, so I actually looked forward to time and space on my own to do a little cooking, or clearing out of cupboards or some domestic annual job that I never got round to.

Fair enough, but before many hours of the day had passed, I began to feel lonely. People weren't even around to chat to on the phone; they were doing special things. If it was an ordinary Thursday or Monday when everyone else was at work, somehow it would have been easier, but to be alone and lonely on a special day was hard to bear.

I still find it so. However, if we are to enjoy later life, it's likely we are going to be on our own for quite a few years, and in later life we don't always have a whirl of social engagements. We couldn't keep up the energy for one thing, and there may be less to do. So how do we cope?

I realise that the holiday gaps in my life are times when I need to clear out the places that are excluded from my weekly house-clean. Perhaps other people don't find crumbs and worse at the bottom of the pile of forks in their cutlery drawer. I bet no–one else found a rather shrivelled dead frog behind their cooker like I did when I pulled it out for cleaning. Oh yes, and the messy business of de-frosting the freezer gets left to the slack times.

A less hectic schedule does mean, however, that there is a spiritual opportunity. Its hard work but I reckon we have to use the time for intercession and praise and generally soaking up Jesus. I find it really hard to do this just sitting still, but with some easy manual occupation to hand, it's the perfect complement.

I enjoy the garden. I'm not someone who delights in all the various species with their Latin names, but I enjoy caring for my plot, creating shapes with the trees and bushes, cultivating all the fruit that burgeons in abundance, and the satisfaction of a newly-mown lawn. So unless I tackle an un-loved cupboard that I haven't investigated for a year or so, there's always the garden, and what a prayer place!

I don't keep myself to a rigorous plan, but ask the Spirit to drop into my mind things to pray about. You may have a different way of doing things. However, if we are single and on our own, we can 'do retreat' without having to go and look for it.

In church house groups I often feel the odd one out. Everyone else is talking about the problem of fitting in times of quiet in an over busy schedule with taking the children to school, going to work, managing the household etc. etc. and I am thinking that I'd like a few more people around the house and a bit more bustle, as I can always choose to have a time of quiet and soak in Jesus.

With imagination, our aloneness can be turned into fruitful activity of various sorts and indeed special times with God. I know some people whose spiritual highs are all connected with their church services and their church outreach. They always want to go and hear this famous speaker or that, to enhance their spirituality and understanding of God's ways. I don't feel the same. Maybe it's because, being the youngest of three, with quite a gap between me and my sister, I've followed a more independent life than most. I notice that the part of my life dedicated to God's service, for example the broadcasting and the writing, are done on my own, rather than in a team.

So in later life and looking forward to possibly twenty more years of later life, when I am alone I must treasure my independence and work at it until it is a truly fruitful part of my existence.

Marie de Hennezel said:

"Working at growing old implies an acceptance of solitude."

We need to work on that acceptance!

I do enjoy good conversation with people. One of the programmes I present on local radio is like a local 'Desert Island Discs' without the island or the celebrity factor. Anyone, yes anyone, who can choose sixteen tracks of music that relate to their life in some way and can make a programme with me. I thought my guests would enjoy doing this, but I never realised what fulfilment I would receive in catching insights into their lives! So I call myself independent by necessity and maybe by background, but I enjoy others around me, and find it quite a discipline being on my own for a whole morning!

Home as a spiritual resource

What I have been learning lately is that the physical area, that I call my home, for me a whole house, for some of you just a room, can be filled with God the Holy Spirit. This is the territory which I am allowed to fill spiritually. We may not experience the dazzling presence of the Lord so bright that we can't face it, as in Moses' time, but we can ask for the Holy Spirit to fill it. We can pray over the entrances, maybe symbolically touch the lintel and sides of the front and back door, to mark the blood of Jesus keeping sin from entering in.

Obviously the Spirit cannot be seen, but we should notice when the Spirit has left the place because of some problem or bad thing that has happened. When in a hotel room, I normally pray in it that any evil that has been left over from previous occupants goes, in the powerful name of Jesus. I ask for the fullness of the Holy Spirit to permeate every part. This enables us to be free from bad dreams. In later life we may be more aware of the spirituality of the place. We might have been walking in the Spirit for some years and be a bit more experienced in this realm.

Last year, at a Summer School where we practised and performed a musical in a week, one of the evening activities was some sort of Japanese drumming. Well I thought that just working at rhythm on drums would be fine spiritually. When they shouted words in another language I called out the name of Jesus, so I thought I was covered. However, the strength of the other religion from which this drumming came was such that I had two bouts of extremely bad nightmares which could hardly be 'outed' through my usual crying out to Jesus.

On another occasion in my own home, just a day or so after my husband had died and gloriously, I believe, been received in heaven, I had a vision that I spied somebody in the porch. I have two front doors with a little porch in between. I opened the door and to my horror saw, what I can only describe as somebody dressed as an angel of death, with a hood but no face and a staff in his hand. I lost no time in banishing this thing from my home, and never after that did I ever feel afraid of the dark, or anything suspicious within my house. I have to say that with my vivid imagination sometimes I used to have tinges of fear, but after this encounter, never again.

As Christians in later life, we can be wise to our surroundings and use all the spiritual resources God has given us. Let's face it, we are made up of our body and mind/soul and the spirit. Our bodies may be functioning less in later life, and though I hope our minds will stay sound, our spiritual function will remain intact. I do believe this. I have taken Christian discussion sessions with those with learning disabilities, both mentally and physically impaired, and even if their minds are not quite right, their spirits are.

Let's use the authority we have in Christ. We can be powerful in his power alone in spiritual things.

I believe that our later life should not be a winding down of all that has made us what we are. It should be leading up to the pinnacle of the crescendo of glorious life which in turn leads to the door into eternity.

Bibliography

Quotes from book by Diana Athill: 'Somewhere Near the End'.

Quotes from book by Marie de Hennezel: 'The Warmth of the Heart Prevents your Body from Rusting'.